Isaac Ferris, Society American Bible

Jubilee Memorial of the American Bible Society

Being a Review of its First Fifty Years' Work

Isaac Ferris, Society American Bible

Jubilee Memorial of the American Bible Society
Being a Review of its First Fifty Years' Work

ISBN/EAN: 9783337099947

Printed in Europe, USA, Canada, Australia, Japan

Cover: Foto ©Lupo / pixelio.de

More available books at **www.hansebooks.com**

JUBILEE MEMORIAL

OF THE

AMERICAN BIBLE SOCIETY:

BEING A REVIEW OF ITS FIRST FIFTY YEARS' WORK.

Prepared by appointment of the Anniversary Committee, and preached in parts, 6th May, 1866, in Presbyterian Church corner 19th Street and Fifth Avenue,

BY ISAAC FERRIS, D.D., LL.D.,

CHANCELLOR OF THE UNIVERSITY OF NEW YORK CITY.

PRINTED BY VOTE OF THE BOARD OF MANAGERS.

NEW YORK:
AMERICAN BIBLE SOCIETY,
BIBLE HOUSE, ASTOR PLACE.

1867.

JUBILEE MEMORIAL

OF THE

FIRST FIFTY YEARS

OF THE

AMERICAN BIBLE SOCIETY.

How intense and how wide spread was the interest of the Jubilee year to the Jewish people! and what a thrill of joy pervaded the masses, as the dawn of such year brought with it releases, restorations—liberations—over the whole land, with all the attendant blessings connected in the Divine arrangement with this remarkable season!

It is not precisely such a year we enjoy; but ours is a year of joy over work accomplished; over blessings diffused through a vast field of want; over spiritual emancipations from the galling yoke of sin; over the shedding of a flood of heavenly light on the sad condition of millions of the benighted, and furnishing to men ready to perish the means of relief. And what has added to the interest of our Jubilee, is the wonderful and long prayed for emancipation of millions living in a state of literal bondage in our land, and the removal for ever of the yoke of slavery, which has distinguished this year.

Its coming has awakened peculiar feelings among our friends over the land, and it is pleasant to note by what appropriate exercises they have commemorated the happy season. At this centre of operations, it has been our privilege to hear from the lips of honoured men, representing various branches of the Christian family circle, of "*the advantages of a written revelation*"—of "*the purity of that revelation*"—of "*the inspiration of the Bible*"—of "*the human and divine in the Bible*"—of "*the Bible and Civil government*"—of it "as *a book for mankind*"—and of "*what it has done for the world the past century.*" We come now to the closing exercises of the contemplated series—which is intended to be occupied with the work done; or, a historical review of the first fifty years of our great National Institution. Though this be not a field for much beside the statement of facts (and hence, perhaps, to the general hearer, of little special interest), yet from that circumstance it has much to interest every friend of the Bible cause. The business aspect of such a great movement must embrace matters of detail; and these illustrate the vitality, the power and efficiency of the Institution—its adaptedness for the great work for which established; the manner in which it has realized the hopes of its founders; but above all, the wisdom and beneficence of the organization—and clearly prove it to have occurred in the fulness of time and under the Divine auspices.

It is recorded, that at the time of the organization an emphatic voice from the midst of the attending audience cried out aloud: "This is none other than the work of the Lord." That which was said then has been often repeated; for every step of our advance shows the Divine hand which laid the foundation; and this, it is thought, we shall see on the present occasion.

The want of a supply of Bibles was deeply and widely felt in the earlier days of our republic, in the midst of its struggle for national life, and various remedial measures were adopted. It is a striking circumstance, that while our fathers were pressed with the burdens and hardships of war, they felt the need of the Bible, and sought to have the people supplied with this best of guides and comforters, and this safest of instructors on their rights and their duties. What a lesson to their descendants! In 1777 a memorial came before the Congress of the Revolution (which had adopted the Declaration of Independence), seeking such relief of the public want at their hands as their wisdom might devise. The application was not flouted at, as if we were a nation without a religion, but proper attention was given to it, and a reference was made of the subject to a committee, who, while they could not provide for the printing, recommended that the government take immediate measures to secure 20,000 copies from Holland, Scotland, or elsewhere, at the expense of Congress.

In 1781—as, in consequence of the war, the English Bibles could not be imported, and when none could tell how long the war might last—on another memorial, a committee reported a recommendation of a Bible printed by Robert Aitken in Philadelphia; on which, the resolution in the following ever memorable words was adopted:

"*Resolved*, That the United States, in Congress assembled, highly approve the pious and laudable undertaking of Mr. Aitken, as subservient to the interests of religion; and being satisfied of the care and accuracy of the execution of the work, recommend this edition to the inhabitants of the United States."

As one well says, "What moral sublimity in this fact, as it stands imperishably recorded and filed in the national archives!—the *first* Congress of the United States assuming the rights and performing the duties of a *Bible society, long before such an institution had an existence in the world!!*"

It was in 1804 when that grand and most memorable event took place, *the organization of the* British and Foreign Bible Society, concerning which our first Secretary, Dr. John M. Mason, said it was "ten thousand times more glorious than all the exploits of the sword;" and of which Dr. Spring has since said, "Old England has no brighter jewel in her crown." The Christian world joins to-day in thanksgiving to God for the worldwide blessings it has diffused and is diffusing. We are happy that her representatives are with us to-day, to participate in our joy, while they bring her most cordial greeting, and that among them is the countryman of him whose earnest appeal for the Scriptures for the Sunday schools and the destitute in the principality of Wales, in 1802, first moved the British heart to the great work which has been accomplished.

The Bible-diffusion spirit was developed early in this century in this country, and with great rapidity after the British movement. The first organization was that in Philadelphia, in 1808; the second, that of the Connecticut State Society in May, 1809; the third, that of the Massachusetts Society in July, 1809; the fourth, that of the New Jersey Society late in the same year; and the fifth, that of the New York (City) Society in 1810. At the commencement of 1816 there were one hundred and thirty-two societies in our country, each independent in its work and entirely local; classified thus:

In New Hampshire	2	In Pennsylvania	15	In Georgia	1
Massachusetts	9	Delaware	1	Ohio	7
Rhode Island	2	Maryland	5	Kentucky	3
Connecticut	2	Dist. Columbia	1	Tennessee	1
Vermont	12	Virginia	12	Louisiana	1
New York	35	North Carolina	1	Mississippi	1
New Jersey	7	South Carolina	2	Indiana	12

Besides these, there were numerous Bible associations.

The supply of the destitution within their own range was all that these societies aimed at, and this was very imperfectly met. It is matter of history, that the Christian heart of our own country was first effectively moved in behalf of the multitudes perishing in the newly and sparsely settled West and South-west, through the agency of one of the devoted band of young men who, in the shadow of the haystack in the meadow near Williams College, planned the Foreign Missionary movement (and gave themselves to it), whose results have been most blessed. Samuel J. Mills, whom we refer to, having completed his theological studies at the Andover Seminary in 1812, was moved, in his large benevolence, at once to undertake a tour of investigation into the spiritual condition of the western and southern parts of the land. He made two tours—the first in 1812 and 1813, in company with the Rev. John F. Schermerhorn, a minister of the Reformed Dutch Church; the second in 1814 and 1815, in company with Rev. Daniel Smith, of the Congregational Church. The correspondence which followed, and the report which was given to the public, of "the nakedness of the land," as regarded the supply of the Sacred Scriptures, awakened the deepest feeling. Mr. Mills, on his return North, visited various cities, and pleaded the cause of the destitute with influential laymen as well as ministers at the most important centres. Very earnest appeals were made in the *Panoplist* (a religious monthly published at Andover, Mass.), at the same time, in behalf of a union of effort in what could only be done by such co-operation; while at the same time urgent exhortations to the same effect came from England, with most glowing accounts of the success of the work in the fatherland.*

* See Appendix (A.)

Early in 1816 the practicability of a great catholic union was illustrated by the organization of two Sunday school Unions in the city of New York—one, in January, of Christian ladies of six or more denominations, under the leadership of Mrs. Divie Bethune, the daughter of Mrs. Isabella Graham; the other of gentlemen, in February, on the same catholic ground, through the influence of Mr. Eleazar Lord.

The excellent Elias Boudinot, then president of the New Jersey Bible Society, made a public communication about this date in favour of a national Bible movement. The New York Bible Society was the first to follow it with formal action, early in the same year, in the adoption of the following resolutions:

"1. That it is highly desirable to obtain, upon as large a scale as possible, a co-operation of the efforts of the Christian community throughout the United States for the efficient distribution of the Holy Scriptures.

"2. That as a means for the attainment of this end, it will be expedient to have a convention of delegates from such Bible societies as shall be disposed to concur in this measure, to meet at on the day of next, for the purpose of considering whether such a co-operation may be effected in a better manner than by the correspondence of the different societies, as now established; and if so, that they prepare the draft of a plan for such co-operation, to be submitted to the different societies for their decision."

These resolutions were transmitted to the president of the New Jersey Bible Society, to be brought before the public if deemed proper.

It was on the 17th of January, 1816, that Mr. Boudinot, then a resident of Burlington, N. J., issued a call, in which he uses this language:

"After mature deliberation, and consulting with judicious friends on this subject, I am decidedly of opinion that the most suitable place for the proposed meeting is in the city of New York, and the most convenient time the second Wednesday of May next, and I do appoint and recommend the said meeting to be held at that time and place."

The Convention accordingly assembled in New York on the 8th of May, 1816, in the consistory or lecture room of the Collegiate Dutch Church, then in Garden Street (where now stand Nos. 50, 52 Exchange Place), under the same auspices which have furnished a place for and established the Fulton Street

Prayer Meeting of our own time, of such blessed memory over the Christian world.

The Convention was composed of sixty members, who represented twenty-eight Bible societies, and were of the Congregational, the Presbyterian, the Protestant Episcopal, the Methodist Episcopal, the Reformed Protestant Dutch, the Baptist churches, and the Society of Friends; and from various sections of our country, east, middle, southern, and western.

They were men of character and of position, every where looked up to with respect and confidence—appreciating deeply the responsibility of their place—entering fully into the work for which they were convened, and taking large views of the results likely to flow from their action—realizing vividly the importance of a truly catholic action. The feeling of interest in their deliberations beyond their circle was intense, and was expressed at the mercy seat in earnest prayer that the Divine Spirit would be their guide, in meetings over our whole country. The occasion was momentous, the scene most solemn. The interchange was free and fraternal. Differences there were, as was to be expected in so novel a movement; but they were happily adjusted, and the result was the adoption of the Constitution prepared by their own committee, by a unanimous vote, and the full organization by the choice of a Board of Managers, and subsequently of the officers, according to the Constitution, at the head of whom was placed the venerable man whose call had convened them, and who regarded the whole action as the most blessed event of his long life.*

Well might the venerable men who took part in these proceedings look back with gratitude on the work done, and rejoice in it in their departing moments. They performed a good service for us and for all coming after us, as they erected a platform on which we may all stand in love and harmony, from whatever tribe of the Christian Israel we come, and may work in unison for the highest good of our common humanity, and prepare for a more blessed co-operation and union in higher services in a better world. How appropriate and how noble the sentiments expressed in the address to the country!—"No spectacle can be

* See Appendix (B.)

so illustrious in itself, so touching to man, or so grateful to God, as a nation pouring forth its devotion, its talent, and its treasures, for that kingdom of the Saviour which is righteousness and peace." All Bible-loving hearts throughout the country were looking anxiously for the final action; and when it came, there ascended the sweet incense of praise from many an altar, and soon there followed large accessions of auxiliaries from all quarters of our land. Thus, the period from the 8th to the 11th of May inclusive, 1816, has become memorable in the annals of the Church of Christ and of the world, as opening an era for good whose range only the revelations of the last day can fully exhibit.

Fifty years have now completed their rapid flight since that memorable occasion, and we have come together to "remember all the way which the Lord our God has led us."

I have assumed that my hearers would desire me to submit to them *a view of the principles which from the first have governed, and still govern, this great National Institution; of the work which has been accomplished; and of the agencies and auspices securing these grand results under God; and what are the prospects for the period to the portals of which a gracious Providence has brought us.*

According to this natural and just expectation, I have arranged the facts I have to submit; and yet I am deeply conscious that the work has been of such vast dimensions, and the interesting details so numerous, that I can furnish mainly summary statements in the time allowed for such an exercise.

My topics are these, viz.:

I. The Principles which have governed and still govern our proceedings.

II. The Work which has been accomplished.

III. The Instrumentalities and Co-operating Agencies which have been enjoyed.

IV. The Prospects which at this point open upon us.

I. THE PRINCIPLES BY WHICH WE HAVE BEEN AND ARE STILL GOVERNED IN OUR WORK.

Let me give these in the simplest form of statement.

1. That which is fundamental and primary is, that *the Bible is a most precious boon to our race.*

It is a most remarkable book, and acknowledged to be such by the ingenuous infidel himself. We join with the historian, the rhetorician, the poet, the painter, and the philosopher, in admiration of this volume as the treasury of what each prizes highly in his special department;* but that on which we fix as making it the most precious boon to mankind, is, that it is the *revelation of a Divine provision for the moral exigencies of our race.*

Two passages of the Sacred Volume sum up the whole: "God so loved the world, that he gave his only begotten Son, that whosoever believeth in him should not perish, but have everlasting life." "This is a faithful saying, and worthy of all acceptation, that Christ Jesus came into the world to save sinners, of whom I am chief."

Man is guilty, and the curse is on him; and destined as he is to another, an eternal state of existence, if he remain as he is morally and spiritually, that curse will abide on him for ever. Hence, the most momentous of all questions are: how shall he obtain pardon? how shall the curse be removed? how shall his immortal state be made one of joy? how shall he be fitted for it and instated in it? The vital value of the Bible is in its answer to these questions; and here is the key to all we have done and would do for its multiplication and diffusion. Can any thing else so worthily occupy the first place in our affections, or more appropriately command all our energies and labours? In man's hopelessness, God has undertaken for him; He "has given his only begotten Son to be the propitiation for our sins; and not for ours only, but for the sins of the whole world." "He who knew no sin was made sin for us, that we might be made the righteousness of God in him." "He suffered, the just for the unjust, that he might bring us to God." "With him is forgiveness of sins and plenteous redemption." "He bore our sins in his own body." "He purged our sins by his own blood;" "and him hath God exalted with his right hand, to be a Prince and a Saviour; to give repentance to Israel, and forgiveness of sins." "There is now no condemnation to them that are in Christ."

* See Eclectic Magazine for July, 1865.

"Being justified by faith, we have peace with God, through our Lord Jesus Christ."

Is there any thing in the whole range of objects which occupy the human mind, or gain the human heart, to be compared with this?

But this is not all. Suppose the guilt be removed; man is *unholy;* his heart is the seat of low and vile affections. Unless he be cleansed, he is unfitted for fellowship with a holy God, or to enter a holy heaven. The Divine provision meets this aspect of the case; for "the blood of Christ cleanseth us from all sin." "God according to his mercy saved us, by the washing of regeneration and renewing of the Holy Ghost." In the Divine economy, it is this Holy Ghost who awakens, enlightens, takes away the stony heart, subdues the pride, implants holy principles in the heart, quickens the soul to the exercise of pure affections, and makes the new creature. Thus begins the meetness for the fellowship with all holy beings and for the coming glory. Thus the blessed Volume presents the good work, which shall be carried forward through the life journey, and it assures us that God is more ready to give his Holy Spirit to them that ask Him than parents are to give good gifts to their children. What can come with sweeter power to the soul struggling with sin than this?

Nor is this all. Man is an *infirm* creature; he is utterly insufficient to make his way onward. The good word for him, accordingly, is: "If any man lack wisdom, let him ask of God, who giveth liberally, and upbraideth not." "I will guide thee with mine eye." "As for the upright, he directeth his way." "To the upright there ariseth light in the darkness." The broad promise is: "I will bring the blind by a way that they knew not; I will lead them in paths that they have not known: I will make darkness light before them, and crooked things straight. These things will I do unto them, and not forsake them," saith the Lord. Is man a feeble creature, unable to cope successfully with the evils, and temptations, and adverse influences which are to be encountered? The provision is: "I will never leave thee, nor forsake thee;" "My grace is sufficient for thee;" "My strength is made perfect in weakness;" "As thy days, so shall thy strength be." So that he may go on cheerily singing: "The Lord is my shepherd; I shall not want: yea, though I walk through the valley of the shadow of death, I will fear no evil: thou art with me; thy rod and thy staff they comfort me." "The Lord will perfect that which concerneth me."

Nor is this all. Man is *poor* and miserable; he can bring no price; personal macerations will be nothing, pilgrimages will be nothing—all manner of penances will be nothing. But the heavenly provision is brought down most happily to his circumstances—all is the *gift* of infinite love: "God so loved the world, that he gave his only begotten Son;" "and with him," the greatest gift, "shall he not freely give us all things?" for these are to Him the smaller gifts.

What a boon is this precious Volume! revealing a provision covering all wants, meeting all exigencies, spreading over all time—all tendered to the guilty, the polluted, the erring, the wretched—of all times and nations—without money and without price. This is our primary principle.

2. The second is this: that it is *God's purpose that this boon should be given to every creature.* If we have examined Dr. Paley's beautiful argument showing design from intelligent adaptation, we cannot but have felt it to be irresistible, as much so as if uttered by an audible voice from heaven. It is so here; there is no chance in the wonderful adaptations of the Book God has given us. There is a purpose in its whole, and in its parts and its every provision. He who knew what man needed has formed it to meet his case. It is clearly for man every where, for he is every where the same guilty, the same helpless, the same polluted, self-destroyed sinner. It matters not what his temporal condition may be, nor in what clime he lives, nor what his relations may be—opening this Book, he finds it a book for him; exposing his heart, arraigning him at the bar, warning him of his danger, insulating him in the crowd around him, holding him firmly to his duty; seemingly written for him specially, and fastening its arrow in his heart. Nothing from human pen is fitted to be so universally a blessing. How can we but conclude it was intended to be such—to go forth as the light, the joy, and the life of the world? The pious heart rejects

with horror as a blasphemy that it could have been made to be the book of only a class, or a nation, or an age. It is the Book of the race.

Besides, how clearly is this contemplated in the Volume itself! Did not the command to preach the Gospel to every creature carry with it the written word, as well as the oral communication, in the necessities of the case? Did not our blessed Lord have this in his mind when he said, "Wheresoever this Gospel shall be preached in the whole world, there shall also this, that this woman hath done, be told for a memorial of her?" Did Luke write only for his most excellent Theophilus? Did not all Christians of the early ages so understand it, as they multiplied copies as far as their circumstances allowed? Did not the enemies of Christianity so understand and fear it, as they sought to make Christians give up the sacred books that they might be burned? Yes; the answer to the inquiry, What was the Divine purpose? is found in the use God has been pleased to make of it—in the remarkable efficiency He has given to it. Where can we look, as we trace the diffusion of the Sacred Word, that we do not see it made the power of God unto salvation? The promise long since given was: "My word shall not return unto me void, but shall accomplish that, whereto I sent it." Through this the blind eyes are opened, the deaf ears are unstopped, the hard heart is melted, the life is reformed, the lost one is recovered, the dead one is brought to newness of life, the servant of sin becomes a child of God, the outcast is made the heir of "an inheritance incorruptible, undefiled, and that fadeth not." The Christian heart is filled with adoring gratitude, as it notes how these blessings confirmatory of his will and desire are multiplied in our day. We are constrained to say, How wonderfully God works!

3. Another grand principle governing our action is, "that this precious boon should be given to men in *its integrity and purity*." It is, as it is in its parts and as a whole, God's Book; and the responsibility is most solemn to give it as God has given it. Modifications, additions, diminutions, destroy this character. The reasoning here is very simple. We owe it *to God* to preserve and diffuse it in its integrity. His honour, his truth, his

purposes concerning it, are all involved here. If we give what He has not given—if we teach what He has not taught—if we claim as his what He has not authorized, we deceive at the expense of his glory and honour; we place ourselves under the condemnation of the false prophets. On the other hand, we owe it to *our fellow men* to maintain its integrity. Their dearest interests are involved here. Can we conceive of any thing more horrible than to delude by giving to the guilty and the dying, as coming from their Maker, what is human—pledging Him to what He has not warranted—raising hopes He has never encouraged—sending them to his bar with a falsified record? How could they guilty of such a course meet God in the judgment, or meet their fellow men at his bar? Will any visitation be too heavy for those who are unfaithful in such circumstances? Those are fearful words with which the Sacred Volume closes: "If any man shall add unto these things, God shall add unto him the plagues that are written in this book: and if any man shall take away from the words of the book of this prophecy, God shall take away his part out of the book of life, and out of the holy city, and from the things which are written in this book." It is true the reference is here specifically to John's prophecy, yet the reason for it applies to all which God has spoken.

4. A fourth principle is this: this blessed boon must, by price and gift, *be brought within the range and circumstances of all.*

Remembering how various are the conditions of men, how vast the proportion unable to buy, how multitudinous the youth whom especially we should seek to guide into the path of truth by an infallible light, how would any other policy have become us, if our aim was to confer the greatest blessings on the greatest number? This is and has been our ground. The American Bible Society is strictly *a benevolent* Institution. It manufactures and disposes of the Scriptures, in no case for the sake of *profit*, but solely for a *philanthropic* and *Christian object.* The Society owes its origin not only to the desire of *cheapening the Scriptures*, so as to bring them within the reach of all classes of persons who possess ability to purchase them, but also to the desire of carrying the Scriptures into retired and destitute parts of the country, where they otherwise never would have been carried; so that all descriptions of persons and all varieties of households might become possessed of them by *purchase or by gift.* In all cases, where the Society *sells* the Scriptures, it does so *at simple cost;* and in all cases, where individuals are destitute, and at the same time are either *unable or unwilling* to purchase, it furnishes them "*without money and without price.*"

5. The last principle governing us which I mention is, that we have been, and are in our work *only stewards and almoners for others.* While our post is one of honour and high privilege, it is one of great responsibility. We are, in all this, in trust for all those who seek by our hands to give the Word of Life to the benighted and the perishing. We are occupants of a peculiarly solemn position. All our distinctions are merged in that highest of all—we are Bible men. Away from this association we may belong to the various tribes of the Christian Israel, but here we are one in our work, in our aim, in our desire. On broad Bible ground we plant ourselves, and for simple Bible ends we labour. The living look to us as their agents, and commit to us their liberal gifts. As such, the widow sends her mite, and the new convert his consecration thank offering; and the churches give, some in their poverty and others of their abundance. But how does this stewardship rise in the solemnity of its character, as we think of the pious dead! Among the last acts of life, ere they passed away to their rest, they remembered the preciousness of God's Word, and they could say, "Thy statutes have been my songs in the house of my pilgrimage," and they recalled how many are without it; they placed in our hands the means of making such happy also—of widening to the world's circumference the circle of human comfort and blessedness by their testamentary acts. Every month there comes to us some touching memento of their regard for the Bible, and new proof of their confidence in our work. It is required of the steward that he be faithful; especially in the stewardship of the mercies of God should it be so. We cannot but heed the voice coming to us from our hosts of living benefactors, of all Christian names and interests; especially can we not be heedless

to the monition coming from the tomb of the deceased—"Be ye faithful."

With this rapid review of principles, we pass—

II. *To a consideration of the work accomplished.* Clearness of presentation leads us to notice here two aspects of the work, viz., *production and distribution;* the former embracing the versions or translations produced in the English and in other tongues; the latter, the diffusion over the home and the foreign field.

1. Our work has had to do with the English version, "that grand old version," as some one enthusiastically and truly calls it. In speaking particularly of this, I will avail myself of the statements made by the Committee of revision in their report, printed 1851:

Besides the translation of Wickliffe, completed about A.D. 1380, but existing until quite recently only in manuscript, six Protestant English versions had been printed and circulated, anterior to the one now in use.

The earliest published English Bible was that of *Tyndale.* The New Testament was printed in Holland, in 1526, and several times afterwards; the Pentateuch at Hamburg in 1530. This version was followed in 1535 by *Coverdale's* translation of the whole Bible; which was twice republished, in 1550 and 1553. *Matthew's* Bible, so called, was printed in 1537, in Hamburg or some other part of Germany. The name Thomas Matthew is understood to be fictitious; and the work seems to have been mainly made up from the translations of Tyndale and Coverdale. According to some, the real editor was the martyr John Rogers.

In 1539 was published *Cranmer's* or the *Great Bible,* in folio, printed at London by Grafton and Whitchurch, king's printers; and hence sometimes known also as Whitchurch's Bible. This was a revision of Matthew's version; and measures were taken to have it kept in the churches and publicly read. Other editions appeared in 1540.

The *Geneva* Bible, so called, was translated at Geneva by English scholars, who had taken refuge there during the reign of Queen Mary. The New Testament was printed at Geneva in 1557; and the whole Bible in 1560. This version was reprinted at London in 1572, and often afterwards.

In 1568 appeared the *Bishops'* Bible, so called, in folio. It was a revision of Cranmer's or the Great Bible, by archbishop Parker and other bishops; and took the place of Cranmer's Bible as the authorized English version.

At the accession of king James I., in 1603, the two versions last named, the Bishops' Bible and the Geneva Bible, were those mainly in use in England;

the former authorized to be publicly read in the churches, and the latter mostly used in private families.

The immediate occasion of the present translation was the celebrated Hampton Court Conference, held before the king, Jan. 12th, 1604. On the second day, Dr. Reynolds, the leader of the Puritans, proposed to the king that there should be a new translation of the Bible, because of the imperfections of the former versions. The king entertained the proposal; with the understanding, that the new version should "last of all be ratified by his royal authority, and so the whole church be bound to this translation, and not to use any other." Accordingly, before the middle of the same year, 1604, the king commissioned a large number of scholars of both the Universities and elsewhere to meet, and consult together, in order to make a new and more correct translation of the Bible. These were divided into *six* classes, comprising forty-seven persons, whose names are given; who were to meet at Westminster, Cambridge, and Oxford, two classes in each place. The original Scriptures, including the Apocrypha, were in like manner divided into six portions; one of which was assigned to each class for translation. Certain rules, prescribed by the king, were transmitted to the translators by the bishop of London, at midsummer, 1604. Among these the following serve to mark definitely the character of the translation and the manner of proceeding:

"1. The ordinary Bible read in the Church, commonly called *The Bishops' Bible*, to be followed, and as little altered as the original will permit.

"14. These translations to be used when they agree better with the text than the Bishops' Bible, viz., *Tyndale's*, *Coverdale's*, *Matthew's*, *Whitchurch's*, [*i. e. Cranmer's*,] *Geneva*.

"6. No marginal notes at all to be affixed, but only for the explanation of the Hebrew or Greek words, which cannot, without some circumlocution, so briefly and fitly be expressed in the text.

"7. Such quotations of places to be marginally set down, as shall serve for the fit references of one Scripture to another.

"8. Every particular man of each company to take the same chapter or chapters; and, having translated or amended them severally by himself where he thinks good, all to meet together, to confer what they have done, and agree for their part what shall stand.

"9. As any one company hath dispatched any one book in this manner, they shall send it to the rest, to be considered of seriously and judiciously."

Besides these forty-seven translators, it appears that "three or four of the most eminent and grave divines of each university" were appointed to be *overseers* of the translations; and these with the others probably made up the number of *fifty-four* mentioned in the king's letter of July 22d, 1604.

After the work was actually commenced, more than *three* years, or, as the original Preface has it, "twice seven times seventy-two days and more," were spent by the several companies in completing the first draft of the new version. When thus far finished, three copies of the whole Bible were sent to London; one from Cambridge, one from Oxford, and one from Westminster. From the companies in these several places, two persons were now selected from each place, *six* in all, who met in London to review the whole work, and prepare one copy from the three, to be committed to the press. Their labours extended through three quarters of a year. "Last of all, Bilson, bishop of Winchester, and Dr. Myles Smith, afterwards bishop of Gloucester, again reviewed the whole work, and prefixed arguments to the several books;" by which "arguments" are probably intended the contents of the chapters, etc. Dr. Smith also wrote the Preface. The translation thus laboriously and faithfully prepared, was first printed and published in A.D. 1611, in folio, and in the old black letter.

In the Preface the translators say: "We never thought from the beginning, that we should need to make a new translation, nor yet to make of a bad one a good one; but, to make a good one better, or out of many good ones one principal good one, not justly to be excepted against, that hath been our endeavour, that our mark." This is doubtless a true and appropriate statement of the object and motives which these eminent persons had before their minds, in executing the great work thus solemnly committed to their charge. They claimed no infallibility for themselves, nor for their labours. The work assigned them was strictly a revision of the Bishops' Bible; which itself had grown up out of all the preceding versions. But they everywhere took the original Scriptures as their basis; diligently comparing likewise all the former translations. In this way they certainly succeeded in making "one principal good translation, not justly to be excepted against." Yet notwithstanding all their care and diligence, their own first edition exhibits some grave errors of the press; most of which were speedily corrected in subsequent editions.

Such was the origin of this venerable and truly national work; which immediately became the standard English Bible, and superseded all the other versions. Confined at first to the limited territory of the British Islands, and intended only for a population of a few millions, it had the effect at once to develope and fix the structure and character of the English language; and with that language it has since been borne abroad even to the ends of the earth. And now, during the lapse of almost two and a half centuries, it has gladdened the hearts, and still gladdens the hearts, of millions upon millions, not only in Great Britain, but throughout North America and India, in portions of Africa, and in Australia. At the present day, the English is probably the vernacular tongue of more millions than any other one language under heaven; and the English Bible has brought and still brings home the knowledge of God's revealed truth to myriads more of minds, than ever received it through the original tongues.

The translators little foresaw the vast results and immeasurable influence of what they had thus done, both for time and for eternity. Venerated men!

their very names are now hardly known to more than a few persons; yet, in the providence of God, the fruits of their labours have spread to far distant climes; have laid broad and deep the foundations of mighty empires; have afforded to multitudes strength to endure adversity, and grace to resist the temptations of prosperity; and only the revelations of the judgment day can disclose, how many millions and millions, through the instrumentality of their labours, have been made wise unto salvation.

The English Bible, as left by the translators, has come down to us unaltered in respect to its *text;* except in the changes of orthography which the whole English language has undergone, to which the version has naturally and properly been conformed; and excepting also the slight variations and discrepancies, which in so long an interval must necessarily arise, by reason of human imperfection, in the preparation and printing of so many millions of copies.

The exposure to variations from this latter source is naturally greater, wherever the printing of the Bible is at the option of every one who chooses to undertake it, without restriction and without supervision; as in this country since the Revolution. In Great Britain, where the printing has been done only under royal authority, by the Universities of Cambridge and Oxford, and the king's printers in London and Edinburgh, the like exposure does not exist in the same degree; although, even there, slight variations are continually manifesting themselves between the copies bearing these different imprints. This will appear more fully in the sequel.

In respect to the *accessories* of the text, comprehending the contents of the chapters, the running heads of the columns, the marginal readings and references, and the chronology, the Bibles of the present day are much less conformed to the original edition. The translators, as we have seen, were to append "no marginal notes at all, but only for the explanation of the Hebrew or Greek words;" and also "fit references of one Scripture to another." To this requirement the early editions were entirely conformed; and the marginal references were very few. In the lapse of time, however, extensive changes and additions have been made in most of the above particulars. The contents of the chapters only have been preserved in the editions of larger size, without very great variation; while in copies of a smaller form, these likewise have been frequently and variously altered and abbreviated.

The following is a brief summary of the periods and editions, in which these changes seem to have been first made:

An edition of king James' Bible was printed in octavo at Amsterdam, in 1664, with a preface by John Canne, a leader of the English Brownists. His purpose was *to make Scripture the interpreter of Scripture*, by the addition of important marginal references "so far as the margin could contain." This edition, with the preface and references of Canne, was several times reprinted by the king's printers in Edinburgh and London. There were editions by them in 1696, 1698, 1701, 1762, 1766, etc.

In England "many parallel texts" were added by Dr. Scattergood, in an edition published at Cambridge in 1678.

Two years later, 1680, an edition was issued at Oxford, with the insertion of Usher's chronology

More important was the Bible published in folio and quarto in 1701, under the direction of Dr. Tenison, archbishop of Canterbury. In this edition Dr. Lloyd, then bishop of Worcester, added the chronological dates at the head of the columns, and a further collection of parallel Scriptures. At the end were also appended tables of Scripture measures, weights, and coins, by Dr. Cumberland, bishop of Peterborough.

This edition was disfigured by typographical errors to such a degree, that the lower house of Convocation, in 1703, made representation on the subject to the archbishops and bishops. But the careless printing of the Bible still continued, and was carried to such a height, in respect both to correctness and paper, that at last complaint was made to king George I. That monarch in consequence issued an order to the patentees for printing Bibles, dated April 24th, 1724, directing that "they shall employ such correctors of the press, and allow them such salaries, as shall be approved from time to time by the archbishop of Canterbury and the bishop of London for the time being." *

At a later period, in an edition published at Cambridge, Dr. Paris made large corrections in respect to the words printed *in Italic.* This fact is mentioned by Dr. Blaney; but we have seen no further account of the edition.

The most complete revision of the English Bible was that undertaken at Oxford by Dr. Blaney, about A. D. 1767, under the direction of the Vice Chancellor and other Delegates of the Clarendon Press. According to his instructions, the Oxford copies were carefully collated with the folio edition of 1611, that of Dr. Lloyd in 1701, and two Cambridge editions of a late date. The work occupied between three and four years; and in 1769 both a quarto and a folio edition were published at the Clarendon Press; of which the folio was supposed to be the most perfect. The editor remarks, that "many errors found in former editions have been corrected, and the text reformed to such a standard of purity, as, it is presumed, is not to be met with in any other edition hitherto extant." The points upon which particular attention was bestowed were the following:

1. The punctuation was revised, in order to express the true sense, and also to insure uniformity, as far as possible.

2. As to the words printed *in Italic*, the Hebrew and Greek originals were compared, and many alterations made. These changes were all submitted previously to the Select Committee, and especially to the Vice Chancellor of Hertford College and Mr. Wheeler, Professor of Poetry.

3. In the heads or contents of the chapters, likewise, considerable altera-

* Thus far the facts respecting the origin and history of the authorized Version have been mainly drawn from Lewis' *History of the several Translations of the Bible into English*, second edition, London, 1739, 8vo. See also the authorities there cited.

tions were made. On these much labour was expended by the editor; as also by the two gentlemen above named, and by Mr. Griffith, of Pembroke College, and the (then) late Warden of New College; by whom the suggestions of the editor were corrected and improved.

4. The running titles over the columns had to be adapted to editions of different size.

5. The Hebrew proper names, where the text contains an allusion to their meaning, were more fully translated in the margin.

6. Obvious and material errors in the chronology were rectified.

7. The marginal references were carefully compared and corrected, and many new ones added, particularly from what is mentioned as a "Scotch edition." The new references are said to have amounted to the number of 30,495, or about *thirty* to each page on an average.*

This edition of the Bible by Dr. Blaney has been regarded, ever since its publication, as the standard copy, to which all subsequent issues in England have been conformed. A beautiful edition in quarto was published in London by Eyre and Strahan, printed by Woodfall, in 1806, and again in 1813. In carrying this copy through the press, it is said that *one hundred and sixteen* errors were detected in Blaney's edition; one of them an omission of some importance.

Your Committee are not aware, that any later general revision or collation of the English Bible has taken place in Great Britain. About twenty years ago, the public mind, in that country and in our own, was for a time agitated by the charge openly made against our present English Bibles, that they had been greatly corrupted from the original edition; and that what we now have is not the English version as prepared by king James' translators. In consequence of this charge, the Clarendon Press issued in 1833, in quarto, an exact reprint in Roman letter of the folio edition of 1611 in black letter. "The reprint is so exact, as to agree with the original edition page for page, and letter for letter; retaining throughout the ancient mode of spelling and punctuation, and even the most manifest errors of the press."

The publication of this reprint tranquillized the public mind; for it presented ocular demonstrations, that, with the exception of typographical errors, and of the changes conformed to, and required by, the progress of orthography in the English language, the text of our present Bibles remains unchanged, and is without variation from the original copy as left by the translators.

Appended to this reprint is a collation made with one of the copies of the year 1613, two years after the original edition. The variations are about 375 in number, exclusive of the Apocrypha. Whether the editions of 1613 were

* The preceding details are taken from Dr. Blaney's *Report to the Vice Chancellor and other Delegates of the Clarendon Press*, dated Oct. 25th, 1769, and printed in the *Gentlemans' Magazine* for Nov. 1769, Vol. XXXIX. p. 517 *sq.* The number of new marginal references is given in the *Encyclop. Metropol.*, art. *Bible.*

printed under the supervision of the translators probably cannot now be known. The variations may be divided into *three* classes, viz., Manifest errors of the press in the copy of 1611; manifest errors of the press in the copy of 1613; other variations from the reading of 1611; but whether with or without design is not always certain.

It was natural, it was an imperative duty, for the Society to secure for its use and publish a Bible as near as possible in conformity with the best, or most correct, English copy. And it was the more necessary that some responsible body should have this in charge, as there was a liability if in the hands of the ordinary printer and publisher, from the very magnitude of the work, to suffer errors to creep in. Some of our American editions from private hands have been sadly defective, while some from high sources should have been more rigidly watched. There is a place here for all the punctiliousness which distinguished the transcription of the Jewish text. Having the best translation extant, it would have been unpardonable to be careless in reproducing it. Ours have not been the times or the facilities requisite to do any thing beyond securing the correctness of the text. Some tyros, with a smattering of linguistic skill, thrust forth their improvements of the translation, as if to impress their hearers with their superior wisdom; and some older heads seem to think their work is to show up the defects of the translation on all occasions, as if they were glaring and numerous; becoming thus auxiliaries of the adversary in undermining the confidence of the plain reader in his Bible. The men who gave us our English translation were giants in their department; their race has not been surpassed, if in individual and rare cases equalled. The distinguished Dr. Guthrie has said: "Our version of the Bible, like the men who made it and those also who use it, is not faultless. It cannot be so; for 'who can bring a clean thing out of an unclean?' The web must ever, more or less, partake of the loom. Still, the good and learned men to whom King James committed the work of translation, take it altogether, have done it well—so well, that all succeeding attempts to produce a better have failed. And perhaps the time and labour which some authors have spent in detecting and exposing the small faults of our version would have been as well employed in correcting the large faults of their own creed and conduct."

Our Society has from the first been jealous on the subject of a correct text, and has employed every means to secure it. In 1847 the Version Committee undertook the most careful revision of our English text in order to secure its conformity to the best British, so as to make what should be a standard edition. This committee consisted of the following gentlemen, viz.: Rev. Dr. Spring, Rev. Dr. Turner, Rev. Dr. E. Robinson, Rev. Dr. R. S. Storrs, Rev. Dr. T. E. Vermilye, Rev. Dr. James Floy, Thomas Cock, M. D. Years of labour and painstaking were devoted to the work; reports of progress were made from time to time, and their final report in 1851. The work at first met with universal favour, and was unanimously approved by the Board; but exceptions having arisen, with considerable excitement, in quarters which the Board felt bound to hear, it was decided to reconsider and modify some things which had been done, and the subject was referred to the same committee; but, in view of all the circumstances, they begged to be excused from the work.* A new committee composed of the following, viz.: Rev. Dr. Spring, New York, Rev. Dr. John N. McLeod, New York, Rev. Dr. H. B. Smith, New York, Rev. Dr. Wm. H. Campbell, New Jersey, Rev. Dr. H. J. Schmidt, New York, Rev. Dr. Wm. R. Williams, New York, Rev. Dr. Lot Jones, New York, Rev. Theodore D. Woolsey, LL.D., Connecticut, Rev. W. J. Lindsay, New York, was appointed for the purpose, and their work, as reported and approved by the Board, is now our standard. Many were satisfied with the first, and all are disposed to yield their confidence to the present.

A by-law of the Board requires that a copy of the first edition of every book it publishes, and a copy of every other edition thereof in which material alterations have been made, shall be placed and preserved in the Library of the Society. The catalogue gives the list of these down to and including 1862; and it thus appears, that of the whole English Bible, seventy-three

* Dr. Spring, in his recent work, "Life and Times," devotes a chapter to this subject. See also Annual Report, 1858.

kinds* have been printed; of the New Testament, thirty-four kinds; of New Testament and Psalms, twelve kinds; of Psalms, three kinds; of portions, viz., of John, one; of Proverbs, two kinds—the differences being in size, in style of type, in the use of references, in marginal readings, in the use of stereotype or electrotype plates, some from plates derived from different sources, and others which are merely technical with the printer—all, however, conformed to the best English text of the date when produced.

Among the facts to be noticed in the production of Bibles in our own tongue, one of the most delightful is that of providing the Sacred Volume in raised letters for the blind. Cut off as they are from innumerable sources of enjoyment which give a zest to life to the seeing, and until our own time from intellectual culture to any great extent; living in perpetual darkness—life a continual night—blessed day was it to them when a Christian humanity discovered a means by which the fields of general culture were opened to them, and especially access was opened to all the riches of the Word of God. Can any one conceive the comfort of one who, with his Bible before him and ability to read it, lives in daily fellowship with all the past, and though the world is shut off from his visual organs, has a world of his own, in which his association is with all that is excellent, in all elevating as well as satisfying themes, and fellowship with the Father and his Son Jesus Christ? How rich such an one now in perpetual day! The printing of the Bible for the blind is one of our most blessed works, costly though it may be. He who doubts it must take his place by the side of the pious blind, and hear the outgushing of his happiness. It has been our delightful privilege to extend this precious boon to the blind in Arabia, Egypt, and Syria.

As to the languages of Europe, the provision of French, Spanish, Italian, German, and Portuguese Scriptures has been a special object. A constant and increasing demand for those at home received very early attention. The standards used have been those deemed in sound judgment to be the most reliable.

* 4to, four; 8vo, twenty-three; 12mo, twenty-three; 18mo, thirteen; 32mo, six, and 16mo, four—none in folio.

In the Spanish, we have reason to believe we have the best version in use, prepared by careful revision at our expense by the hand of a most cultivated native of Spain,* who under our roof has devoted years to its preparation. But in our work on the continent, most has been and must be accomplished by subsidies of money to native societies and agencies. It is to us a pleasant fact, that the new world is thus reflecting to the old countries the light which came from them; and the land which has most successfully perfected the printing press sends back its bounty to the land in which the art of printing was invented, and the Bible in Latin was first printed.

One of the efforts of our first year was to provide for the wants of the aborigines of our country, and it has always been kept in view. In the course of years, portions have been furnished for the Mohawks, the Delawares, the Senecas, the Ojibwas, the Dakotas, the Choctaws, the Cherokees, the Shawnees.

As we proceed to speak of the Scriptures (in whole or in part) in Eastern and African tongues, it is becoming to note emphatically our indebtedness to missionaries, without whose aid nearly two thirds of the human family must have been left without the Word of Life. These noble, self-sacrificing men, selected for their work with great care by the Church, well furnished by literary training, have performed a service in the departments of ethnology, philology, and geography, involving the physical, civil, and social condition of the people of other lands, which has made general science very much their debtor.† Their circumstances constitute them the best authorities in all these matters. Not travellers, and thus almost constantly in transit, and only seeing the outside of things, or the mere dioramic, swiftly passing scenes of life—but living among the people in familiar, intimate, confiding intercourse—they are qualified both to know the wants of the people, in religious things especially, and to learn the best mode of meeting them. Acquiring living tongues among the people who use them, they early feel the need of the printed Volume, and are the

* Professor De Mora, of the University of the city of New York.

† Since the above was written, an able article on this subject has appeared in the Princeton Review for October, 1866.

men to prepare it. With all their previous careful preparation in the best literary and theological institutions of Christian lands, who rather than they can be confided in?

That noble institution, the British and Foreign Bible Society, has published the Bible in one hundred and sixty-nine languages and dialects, and for the larger proportion of these is indebted to English and American missionaries.

That is a most memorable record given by the venerable secretary of the American Board of Commissioners for Foreign Missions of the work of its missionaries in the department of Christian literature and Bible translation in pagan tongues. He says: "The number of languages in which books have been printed at the presses owned by the Board is forty-three, viz.: the modern Greek, Hebrew, Spanish, Armenian, Turkish, Bulgarian, Arabic, Syriac, Mahratta, Gujerattee, Sanscrit, Hindustanee, Portuguese, Persian, Tamil, Telugu, Siamese, Malay, Bugis, Dyack, Chinese, Japanese, Hawaiian, Marquesas, Micronesian, Grebo, Mpongwe, Dikèlè, Zulu-Kaffir, Cherokee, Choctaw, Creek, Osage, Ojibwa, Ottawa, Seneca, Abenequis, Sioux or Dakota, Pawnee, three in Oregon."

Our Board early understood the value of missionary aid, and adopted resolutions encouraging the preparation of versions by missionaries in all fields. To the various missionary stations these were their expressions: "The Managers look with peculiar satisfaction on the efforts of American missionaries, of different religious denominations, in translating the Scriptures into the various tongues and dialects used at their respective stations; that they hope to receive intelligence whenever the Old Testament, or the New Testament, or any one entire Gospel or other book of the Bible, is correctly translated and ready (without note or comment) for the press; and that the missionaries be encouraged to expect that, on giving intelligence, they shall receive the aid requisite for the publication of the same." Thus have we been furnished with a variety of translations, in a number of cases where, previous to the labours of the missionaries, the languages had not been reduced to writing, the general rule governing the preparation of such versions being, "that they should conform to the common English version; at least, so far as that all religious denominations represented in the American Bible Society can consistently use and circulate said versions in their several schools and communities."

This was the great foundation principle of our Union, put into written form, without which it could not have been formed, and now could not exist. This met the decided approbation of all the denominations in the Bible Society compact, excepting a portion of the Baptist brethren, from two of whose mission versions help was withheld in consequence of their denominational character. The action gave offence to those brethren, and they separated from us; while some notable representative brethren of the same communion aided in shaping the final action of our Board in the circumstances, and have always maintained that the course pursued was the true and only one for the National Institution under its Constitution. Let me say, by the way, time works material changes; and when excitements die out, and calm revision takes place, it is pleasant to know that the place at the common board is kept unoccupied, and the door to its occupancy stands open, on the ground of the catholicity of 1816, overarched by the inscription,

——"WELCOME ALL WHO LOVE OUR LORD JESUS CHRIST."——

Under this policy the Board have been enabled to furnish the Scriptures, in whole or in part, in the following languages and dialects beyond the limits of our own land, and among pagan people: to the Arrawack in South America, to the Hawaiian Islands, the Hindu, Hindi, Urdu, Zulu, the Shikh, the Hindustanee, the Tamil, the Telugu, Creolese, the Syriac, the Arabic, Micronesian Islands, the Esthonian, the Benga, the Grebo, Fuh-Chau Colloquial and Mandarin Colloquial, the Armeno-Turkish, and now it has in course of preparation the Slavonic and the Bulgarian. That which is destined to become the great foreign work of the Board, and is already in progress, is the production of the plates for printing the Scriptures for the vast Arabic-speaking people—"a population extending from Morocco and Timbuctoo on the west, beyond Calcutta on the east, and numbering at least one hundred and twenty millions." It is an interesting fact, that in the Bible House, in the heart of this busy, bustling city, not noticed by the passing throng, this work of preparation is noiselessly going on, and the instrumentality is daily advancing, which shall be a guide and a comfort to our fellow men over a field almost parallel to the English-speaking area in extent, and embracing millions more than speak any one tongue. From missionary hands we receive it, and by missionary hands it is to be accomplished.

Of that version it is proper to add, its preparation occupied *sixteen* years of almost consecutive labour. The Syrian Mission of the American Board of Commissioners set apart for its accomplishment its best men, and to these were added the best native talent which could be procured, in order that it might be conformed to the native style of expression, and to the highest standard of literary taste. Rev. Dr. Eli Smith, regarded as a master of the Arabic, began and advanced the work so far as to complete the translation of Genesis and Exodus, and prepare the basis of a translation of the New Testament, the balance of the Pentateuch, and several minor prophets; and his compeer of equal scholarly rank, Rev. Dr. Van Dyck, completed it. To test its excellence and unsectarian character, each sheet of the translation, before being finally printed, was submitted to the careful scrutiny of every member of the mission, to interested native scholars of all sects, to other American missionaries, to English, German, Scotch, and Irish missionaries of different religious denominations and in different parts of the empire, and finally received the warm and unqualified approbation of all.

Its style of execution is that of a perfect transcript of the Arabic caligraphy of the Koran, according to a mode designed by Dr. Eli Smith, and executed by Mr. Homan Hallock, of the Mission—so delicate, so distinct, so beautiful, that the most captious Mohammedan who regarded with prejudice and as a profanation the printing of sacred books receives it with delight.

Highly is our Board honoured by having charge of the production of this great work, which is destined to produce effects in the Mohammedan world, no one can calculate. It is delightful to see here the American Bible Society linked in "with the grandest operations and results of missionary enterprise." Next in urgency to the supply of our home want will come the widest diffusion of the Arabic version in our next semi-century. But here we shall have co-labourers, in the British and Foreign Bible Society, to whom a set of the plates will be sent, and the vastness of the work will be worthy of both.*

It should be stated that the American Bible Society, in its work of production of books, has not been restricted to plates of its own preparation, but uses those also produced by foreign Bible societies, and especially the British and Foreign Bible Society—presenting thus a union of effort for an end truly common to all and worthy of all. As in union there is strength, with God's blessing we anticipate a much more efficient performance of the work.

To the Arabic, it is to be hoped may soon be added as perfect a version in the Chinese—that a purer light may be shed on that remarkable and multitudinous people, and all may unite in its diffusion.

2. *The distribution* which has been made after this preparation naturally follows. Its beginning was small, very small. Three sets of plates, octavo, and three in 12mo, were donated to the Society by the New York Bible Society and the New York Auxiliary Bible Society, and with these in use, 10,000 of the 12mo were printed, and 6,000 sold, and a further impression of 2,500 8vo and 7,500 of the 12mo ordered, an unusual movement then; but it was the rill which has become a vast river.

Our city has been designated a distributing reservoir, our Institution has been so in the pouring out of the precious Word of Life. In this respect, a reservoir of pure water—most abundant, refreshing, free, adapted to purify, to nourish and strengthen, to allay the thirst of the parched heart—to quench the fire of sinful passion—to cure the sorrows of the soul, and through a thousand ramifications to convey its blessings to every house, to every condition of life, to every age, to all where needed free, and in all its supply increasing as years have passed on. Could they who were constrained to declare their inability to meet the demands of a score of societies in 1816 now hear the Jubilee report, amazement would fill their hearts.

* See Appendix (D.)

Let me present this great work by decades:

	Vols.		Vols.		Vols.
1st year........	6,410	11th year......	71,621	21st year.......	206,240
2 "	17,594	12 "	134,607	22 "	158,298
3 "	31,118	13 "	200,122	23 "	134,937
4 "	41,513	14 "	238,583	24 "	157,261
5 "	43,246	15 "	242,183	25 "	152,202
6 "	53,470	16 "	115,802	26 "	257,066
7 "	54,805	17 "	91,168	27 "	216,605
8 "	60,439	18 "	110,832	28 "	314,582
9 "	63,851	19 "	123,236	29 "	429,092
10 "	67,134	20 "	221,694	30 "	483,873
	439,580		1,549,848		2,510,156

				Totals.	
31st year......	627,764	41st year.....	770,057		
32 "	655,066	42 "	712,045	1st 10 yrs.....	439,580
33 "	564,726	43 "	721,095	2 "	1,549,848
34 "	633,395	44 "	753,772	3 "	2,510,156
35 "	592,432	45 "	721,878	4 "	6,772,338
36 "	666,015	46 "	1,093,842	5 "	10,138,044
37 "	799,380	47 "	1,259,117		
38 "	815,399	48 "	1,425,147		21,409,966
39 "	749,896	49 "	1,530,563		
40 "	668,265	50 "	1,150,528		
	6,772,338		10,138,044		

The British and Foreign Bible Society, organized 1804, has issued 47,989,579 volumes.

The most interesting of questions is, how have these productions of the Bible press been dispensed—by what channels have they been conveyed to their destined fields?

The *auxiliaries* of all grades have borne the principal part. It has been the preferred policy of the Board to secure their organization over the whole country, even to the hamlet, the boarding school, and the juvenile association, embracing both sexes and all conditions of social life. The grand principle involved, is that of bringing home to the heart of every locality over our land the wants of those around it, and to cherish the feeling of responsibility in reference to the improvement of their moral condition, and binding their own attachment to the Word of Life. It has been found most happy, and has diffused the life of the centre to the extremities. The work in the hands of these auxiliaries has been primarily local, but beside this, many have helped on the effort to give the Word to the destitute in other fields. In dealing with the auxiliaries, the practice has been to encourage all possible energy by selling to them at cost, and when needed, to add a grant or gratuity which might more effectually secure the accomplishment of their plans. The invariable practice is, to honour the auxiliary by putting into its hands every call for books from its region, and to make it the agency for any general work it may be able to perform. To secure vitality and call out energy, and make the auxiliary a constant blessing, are ends gained, while the poor have the sacred volume more certainly placed in their hands through their friends and neighbours. These organized channels, with the branches and various forms of association, these conduits of blessings, have risen to the number of 5,232, and last has been added to them two auxiliaries of coloured persons in Tennessee. Sometimes, at the extremes of our population, the Bible Committee, consisting of several trustworthy persons, is the temporary substitute for the auxiliary, and does its work until a more permanent organization occurs.

In dispensing the gratuities of the Society, the Committee of Distribution has a most blessed part to perform—one which constitutes its service a source of positive Christian enjoyment. It is its province to look carefully into every application and recommend the donation which may be needed. Its monthly record discloses the channels through which our benefactions flow forth. Beside the work by the auxiliaries, now the applicant is the Christian traveller, who is about to go forth over a wide and new field, who would take a supply which he may dispense; and then, it is the commercial agent who, while moving variously on his secular work, would do a work for the souls of the strangers with whom he may be thrown. Now, it is the Christian female on the borders of the land who sees many doors opened for Christian usefulness, and earnestly calls for the Bible or portions of it. Then it is the clergyman who is about to try the dangers of the deep and seek a foreign land—who would have the means of doing good to the sturdy mariner on his voyage, and also carry the Scriptures to benighted populations where the light is excluded; then, it is the public functionary going abroad, who, with a warm Christian heart, would have the means of putting into the hands of his wandering countrymen the Bible, which shall remind them of home, while he may help also the stranger. The invalids seeking health in a Southern clime have carried with them many a Bible to the destitute. The pious sea captain has considered it indispensable to take his Scriptures in various languages to deposit at the points where they may do good, and set up in some hearts the fear of God. The Christian family in its summer wanderings has been cast into neighbourhoods where sad destitution prevailed—or where a struggling Sabbath school effort was in progress—or where a feeble Church could, only with great individual sacrifices, sustain the public worship of God; and their appeal must be met. These are the smaller channels; but how pleasant, and often touching!

But on a broader scale: The Tract Society with its vast and most useful colporteur system has been made the conveyancer of many thousands of copies where no other Christian visiter had come. The Parent Sunday School of our country, in its care for the interests of the children, and especially in our newly settled country and where it has often preceded the Church, makes its annual appeal; and no less earnest are the denominational Sunday school unions. The supply of Sunday schools every where among the poor has been an object very near to the heart of the Bible Society. The appeals from the Orphan Asylum, the Penitentiary, the Prison, the Hospital, the Soldiers' Home, the Home of the Friendless, have been promptly heard and answered.

Some periods of revived Bible effort have occurred, which have imparted new energy to our work. In 1825, the Monroe County Bible Society, in our State, solemnly resolved to supply within a year all the destitute families within its limits; and the pledge was redeemed. Many other county societies caught the same spirit and followed the example, and thus, in the progress of a few years, a vast diffusion occurred. But our home supply, in consequence of the rapid changes constantly taking place, and the coming in of new populations, can never be complete, or remain so; hence, many auxiliaries have repeated once and again their good work.

A few years after the county movement, which illustrated what could be done where there was a union of will and effort, the supply of the whole country in two years was undertaken. It was a great national movement, and in the lapse of the time specified, from which the supply was undertaken at differing points, a fair accomplishment of the resolution was publicly announced.

But it was left for the closing five years of our half century to witness the mightiest achievement in the way of home distribution. The unhappy civil strife still fresh in our memory, and whose sad mementos are every where, called our hundreds of thousands from their homes over our whole land. Every feeling of humanity and religion pleaded for every care and provision for their welfare, and especially that they might have the Word of Life. Our auxiliaries did a noble work in their fields—but the needs often exceeded their ability—hence, they appealed for help, that every soldier might carry about him a spiritual comforter and guide. The appeals were heard, the grateful pressure increased, and it was found desirable to adopt a system which should both facilitate the supply and distribute it most wisely. Points were selected to which Bibles and Testaments should be sent, and from which responsible hands should carry them to the army and navy. The system was of such a character and proved so successful as a basis, that it deserves a place here:

I. To the Washington City Bible Society, for the army in Virginia, hospitals, camps, prisons, and within their range of general operations.

II. For St. Louis, for use of the Christian Commission, and for distribution from that point.

III. To the Louisville, Ky., Bible Society, to be distributed, under the supervision of Mr. W. H. Bulkley, its depositary, from that point down into Tennessee, Mississippi, and Alabama.

IV. To the Maryland State Bible Society, for the army hospitals, forts, and ships of war, in and around Baltimore, in Maryland, at Fortress Monroe, and in adjacent parts of Virginia.

V. To the New York Branch of the Christian Commission, for a similar distribution at and near Newbern, North Carolina, and parts adjacent.

VI. To the same, for distribution in the same way at and near Beaufort, South Carolina, and other parts of that State.

VII. For New Orleans, to be under the charge of a special Agent to be appointed, who shall supervise the distribution from that great centre, and who shall, as far as may be practicable, co-operate with such gentlemen of the Southwestern Bible Society as may be disposed to act in concert, and the Christian Commission.

Immediately liberal appropriations were made. The first under the arrangement amounted to 475,000 volumes. From that time every power of our producing department was placed under requisition, and kept so for three full years in succession. We look back with astonishment on the capabilities of our arrangements for furnishing the supply required. The following general statement will aid in the formation of a fair conception of them. During the pressure of 1863, 1864, and a part of 1865, we were enabled to produce, ready for distribution, an amount which was equal to *ten* volumes per minute, embracing all sizes and parts. The Society enjoyed the hearty co-operation of its friends, whose liberality abounded; its agencies were happy to do the work with which they were charged. It was unparalleled in the history of wars, as was that of the Sanitary and Christian Commissions. To the Christian Commission, composed of volunteer labourers from the ministry, the college fraternity, the theological seminary, the counting room, the home circle, the sons and the daughters of the Christian family, we and our country cannot be too emphatic in our thanks, as theirs was a work of the highest Christian benevolence, ministering to the bodily comfort of our brave soldiers, but especially to their soul's welfare, in circumstances of great danger on the battle field, and under various exposures and hardships, in the camps and hospitals, on the land and on the sea. Through this channel were distributed 1,466,748 volumes, valued at $179,824 99. Theirs and ours has been the joy to know that the most blessed fruits accompanied and followed the united Christian services. The whole constitutes a model chapter in the history of evangelical benevolence. The wise ordering of Providence enabled us thus to reach many a man who had not been within our reach before, to revive the heart of many a true Christian soldier, to impart comfort to many a dying brave, and with the survivors, to send many a copy of the Scriptures to homes in the wilderness, and these made dearer by the circumstances in which obtained.

But it was not alone *our* army which was supplied. Large appropriations were cheerfully made to those in conflict against us. And, we are happy to record that our proper authorities unhesitatingly and cheerfully allowed our Bible benefactions to cross the lines to their destinations, and granted liberal use of various public means of transportation.

Closely in connexion with these, where our arms were successful, the Scriptures were sought for and sent through various missionary societies to the freedmen of the South, whose thirst for the precious Word was one of the happiest comments on their appreciation of their changed situation.

It is pleasant to note here, that while our own armies at home were receiving the Scriptures so eagerly, our Agent in Germany was widely distributing them among the Austrian army in the war with Denmark; following thus the example of the lamented Righter, who, in time of the Crimean war, was greatly successful in giving the Scriptures to portions of the British army.

The *missionaries* of the several foreign missionary organizations of our country have constituted another most important channel of distribution. Having furnished in many cases the translations required, they have become the means of supply to vast multitudes who were without the Sacred Word. In many cases, the entire work of preparation and printing has been done abroad on appropriations by our Board; while in others, the Scriptures have been sent from this country. Though distinct in our organizations, the missionary and Bible societies of Christendom become thus by mutual, and we may say, necessary co-operation in the grandest efforts of Christian philanthropy, a WORLD moving agency for good. In the use of this agency in distribution as well as preparation, the Board have been governed by the following views:

1. They can pay for printing and binding of the Scriptures.

2. They can pay for storage of books when needful, and also for their transportation to places of distribution.

3. They can pay for such native colporteur service by believers in the

Bible as they may from time to time authorize and appoint, and as is confined to the distribution of the Scriptures, and when the missionaries have not time to perform this work for themselves.

4. They may appoint, to aid in making and correcting foreign translations, persons of competent learning and skill; such translations or corrections, when prepared and made, to be subject to the action and decision of the Committee on Versions and the Board, as is required by our by-laws.

What, then, is the sum of this half-century diffusion? Upon our own land our abundance has been poured out freely and liberally, and constantly flows on. The aborigines of our country, so rapidly passing away, have been cared for. They who go down to the sea in ships, and do business on the mighty deep, have received the Word at our hands, and been made our carriers of blessed treasures to the islands of both the great seas on the east and west of us. We have planted ourselves on the great continental peninsula south of us, and occupied posts in New Granada and Venezuela on the north; at Rio and Buenos Ayres on the east, sending the Scriptures up the mighty Amazon, and the Lesser Orinoco, and the La Plata, into the interior of Brazil and Buenos Ayres and Argentine Republic; on the west, at Valparaiso in Chili, and at Lima in Peru. Soon may the converging lines meet on the great central plateau! With hearty co-operation we have sent our aid to Bible brethren in sunny France, and multiplied the sources of healthful Christian life among the millions of disenthralled Italy. We have been repaying the Reformation debt to the masses of Germany, sadly corrupted by an infidel virus. Early we sent to Russia the testimonials of our interest in her vast populations. In Greece, over Turkey in Europe, and in Asia, where American missionaries have gone, have they diffused the Scriptures, in whole or in part, which American piety furnished. Down the West African coast, and to various interior tribes, and around to the Natal country, the printed message of mercy has been sent in their own tongues. Over India have our brethren, in our name, dispensed the precious substitute for the Shasters and Zendavesta in various tongues. China, with her dense masses, has to a degree received the Word in her own tongue, while at the door of Japan the missionary is watching the opening, to take in with him at every commercial port his recent translation.

Truly the sun does not set on the immense area to which, and through which, the American Bible Society, as the distributing reservoir of one form of American Christian liberality, is sending the pure water of life to the millions upon millions of immortal men. "Not unto us, O Lord, not unto us, but unto thy name be all the praise, for thy mercy and thy truth's sake."

III. Let me ask your attention now to a third important point, viz., *The facilities and co-operating agencies which have been enjoyed.*

Where so great a work has been accomplished, we naturally decide there must have been instrumentalities adapted to secure the results reported, and these a gracious Providence has furnished us.

1. In the enumeration here to be made, a *first* and special place must be given to the *form* and *character* of our organization. Ours is a catholic institution; and this has imparted to it a special charm and attractiveness. Ours is a union of interests and feelings and efforts. We occupy the ground common to all who love our Lord Jesus Christ. We have no Shibboleth in our relations here. On our frontal is the whole Bible—the open Bible—the unshackled, free Bible. How this at once shuts out agitations, anticipates and prevents jealousies, secures confidence, developes love, gives power, and wins for it a way among all, and a place in the hearts of all! We often hear brethren in public remark and dwell on the catholicity of our platform. We wonder not; for there is a charm in it. Our Divine Master has taught us all a most blessed lesson hereby—that we are one in the same Saviour, and can walk together in the same consecrated way. We are not parted off into narrow inclosures; we are like society itself, where there are family interests and acts separate and peculiar, but where the aggregation constitutes a united whole, and all co-operate for the innumerable common interests in which we are alike sharers. Our union has thus been a most persuasive appeal—a most elo-

quent and moving fact; it has been a moral lever; it has been a key to unlock hearts; and it must ever be so.

It is written indelibly on our Constitution, as expressed in one of the Annual Reports: "We superintend the concerns, not of a party, but of the whole body of Christians, who are united in the National Institution for the sole purpose of distributing the Bible without note or comment." While this has been such an arm of power in "Bible work," it is a delightful thought that its influence has been most widely felt in other relations. There has been a growing feeling of regard towards each other among Christian bodies, and efforts for closer union are the happy characteristic of our times. Where now are those bitter, acrid, injurious, unkind presentations of the opinions of others, which in days past have been so common, and which gave the world only the ideas of contention and sectarian hatred, to the prejudice of piety as being both unlovely and undesirable? Men have learned to respect each other more, and to estimate at a proper value both the points in which they agree and in which they disagree, and to recognise in each other, notwithstanding various differences, followers of the same Saviour, and co-workers in the same great Cause. May the blessed influence go on, until we shall all feel how truly we are one!

2. I mention as a *second* most important agency, in our successful and advancing work, the obtaining of a *local habitation.* We look back, and note with surprise how the conception and plans for a National Institution were in contrast with the means at hand. There was here an infancy which feels its way to strength and progress. It is recorded, that "our Board commenced its work without a home; it lived on hospitality. It expresses its gratitude to the governors of the New York Hospital, and also to the mayor of the city of New York, for their kindness, promptly tendered, in granting them the use of rooms in which for some time they transacted business," and at the time of this expression was accommodated by the New York Historical Society. Its first place of deposite for books was in the office of its Agent, John E. Caldwell, Esq., at the corner of Nassau and Cedar Streets; then in a rear room, seven feet by nine, in the printing office in Cliff Street; then in a building in

Sloat Lane, now Hanover Street, adjoining the Merchants' Exchange, in a rear room twenty feet square (which it was *hoped*, as a great point, would at length be filled); and then its work and depository were in different places. As labour increased, it was felt to be exceedingly inconvenient, and a bar to progress, to have work done in different buildings, and with little security, and an increased risk of incorrectness. The fourth year found the Board necessitated to seek a building which should supply the accommodations requisite for the several departments, and entirely under the oversight of the General Agent. Soon after the sixth anniversary, a proper site was secured in Nassau Street (now Nos. 115–119), and the building was completed by the ensuing winter. Its internal arrangements were well adapted to the purposes of the Society; it was three stories high and fifty feet front, and ran back to Theatre Alley a depth of one hundred feet, contracted at its west end to a width of thirty feet. All the business of the Society was done there, and for the time being it was practicable to carry on the growing business with greater regularity and system, and maintain the proper supervision of each branch of work. Immediately new tone was imparted to every form of work, and greater interest given to the meetings of the Board in a capacious hall. Such was the inflowing prosperity, however, that in 1830 two additional lots adjacent were bought and occupied by buildings, making a front of ninety-four feet on Nassau Street. Here was a property, devoted exclusively to Bible work, worth over $30,000, which private Christian liberality had erected and paid for. It was at the time the most noble benefaction which could have been made. The influence was felt throughout the whole circle of our Bible friends, stimulating to new effort on their part.

Great as was this work then, the enlarged blessings vouchsafed in the lapse of twenty-four years constrained the Board to make an effort for accommodations for operations bearing some proportion to the calls for the Word of Life.

After much inquiry and numerous discouragements, the most desirable spot, where now stands the Bible House, was purchased (containing three quarters of an acre), and the building erected; an object of increasing interest throughout our land. Simple in its style, yet imposing in its noble dimensions, looking over this vast city and central to its teeming population, it cannot but be admired, every inch of it admirably adapted to its purposes, and reflecting the greatest credit on the Committee charged with its erection, and so constructed as to become a large annual contributor to Bible work. While we admire this noble edifice for its architectural beauty and its benevolent aim, we are not to forget that it is also the result of the gifts of private munificence, costing over a quarter of a million, and now estimated as worth more than $350,000.* It stands a glorious testimonial of the largeness of views and wise estimation of the immense uses for which it was to be employed. Its erection is a beautiful illustration of a far reaching faith, whose correctness every year is confirming. After being paid for, the rental of parts not needed for our work yields to the general income of the Society a sum sufficient to pay the salaries of the executive officers. Without the first building, the Society's work must have been sadly dwarfed, and increased calls could not have been encouraged; and yet that building, so valuable in its erection, in our progress proved very deficient. Without the present house, or one equivalent, the work of the last five years could not have been undertaken. Overwhelmed by the pressure, we must have given up in despair of ever meeting the most remarkable opportunity of Bible circulation, providentially furnished at our door, which will scarcely offer again. For the future, we have in it a most suitable preparation. Trusting and believing that God has still greater designs to accomplish by the Society, we may rejoice that our noble House will be ready for them.

3. That the Board have been able to avail themselves of every *typographical advantage*, we mention as a *third* notable circumstance in helping on the Bible work.

The printing of the Sacred Scriptures for our use was done for a number of years by contract, and with the exception of two years, by one house. This system was after the usage of the British and Foreign Bible Society, and has its advantages

* See Appendix (D.), description of building.

and serious disadvantages. When the time of renewal of the last contract had arrived, the whole policy was referred to a Special Committee, composed of the most practical men in the Board. The decision was not arrived at in haste. Every proper inquiry was made; printing and publishing firms were consulted; the report submitted presented the merits of the question fairly, and was adopted by the Board of Managers, January, 1844. The general views of the report deserve a place here, as the whole mode of proceeding by the Society was altered from this date. The conclusions were: "That the Society can do the press work at one half the present prices. There will be a saving over the present system in paper. Having the printing under our own control, we should avoid all collisions with the printer as to the quantity of paper required for a given edition; as to the character of the ink, the manner of pressing the sheets, of the delivery of the work and other minor matters, about which such collisions have not been unfrequent, and which are very unprofitable.

"We should be free from all ground of complaint of paying extravagant prices to our printer, with which some portions of our community have ever abounded, to the injury of our Bible cause, and which our agents are now constantly meeting; for whatever money might be saved by adopting this course would be directly for the advancement of the great cause of the Bible, and not, as now, for the benefit of the individual. This with your Committee is a consideration of great moment." This formed an epoch in the career of the Society, the wisdom of which the successful course of twenty years has most satisfactorily manifested. The Managers were happy in obtaining a suitable superintendent of its printing department, and it at once introduced such improved processes as the advance of the art brought within its reach.

Of the great arts of life, scarcely any branch has been more improved than printing; in the machinery employed, in typography, the saving of composition by the use of plates, while the capability and rapidity of production have increased many fold. Of all this the Managers have been enabled to avail themselves in their former house to a degree, but especially in the present. The use of simple type, of the hand press, has been a marvel in its day, and so was the stereotype. The facility of taking impressions, and of multiplying them to many thousands, and still keep the face of the plates perfect, enabled the printer to meet almost any demand. In our own case, it enabled the Board always to keep in advance of all demands, or meet them at short notice. From a set of stereotype plates, the large number of 350,000 impressions could be taken before they were considered unfit for use.

In 1854, that greatest marvel of printing plates, the electrotype, was first used in the Bible House. Since which, 35,000 electro plates have been made. The amazing fact has been given me, that since April, 1856, three sets of pocket Testament electro plates have been worn out in the service, from which 4,632,000 impressions have been made, being an average of 1,544,000 copies from each.

The Printing Press has also reached a point of almost vitalized power. There are in the press-room fifteen (Adams') power presses, capable of printing nearly 2,000,000 of the Scriptures in a year, while provision has been made in the construction of the press-room to increase the capability of printing one third.*

Let one look at the issues, and he sees the result of the work, and says, How can this be? Let him look at these electrotypes and steam presses, and he can answer his question, but it will be with a feeling of surprise at the wonderful combinations involved. What ability lies here to meet any amount of requisition! Some one has said: "No family in the land need be a day without the Bible, if the auxiliaries are faithful." Happy day will it be when this Society is put to the test of supplying the Scriptures to meet such a movement. The history of the past clearly shows how it will come up to such a new but most desirable condition of circumstances.

4. A constant and increasing supply of *pecuniary* aid by the lovers of the Bible is to be gratefully mentioned as a vital agency in the work accomplished.

Money has been called the sinews of war; so is it of every

* Provision has been made for the introduction of four additional power presses of the largest size. These have been ordered, and two are already in operation.

practical business operation of life. Armies cannot be raised and sustained without it; the affairs of commerce cannot be carried on without it; the State cannot be maintained without it; no more can the great operations of Christian benevolence be carried on without it. Some seem to think that prayer is all that is necessary here, and their means are saved for other purposes. Blessed be prayer; but especially blessed in the divine record is the case of him whose prayers and alms, or practical benevolence, came up in unison before God. We have reason to believe that this union has existed in many a case in our history. While the sincerity of the prayer has been attested by the gift, the efficacy of both has been attested by the crowning, responding blessing which has been poured out.

During the first year the Board, if not startled, were much moved by the rush of calls for the Scriptures while their treasury was low. Accordingly, in addition to all the circulars issued over the land, arrangements were made to have this city districted, and collectors go from house to house to solicit contributions. If there were any fears for the incoming of means, they were soon allayed; for men's hearts and purses were opened, and thousands were emulous to give something for the diffusion of this best of books. The venerable bowed down with years gave, and the child emptied his box of savings. There have been many noble benefactors, to whom it has been a delight to contribute of their abundance; and the widow's mite, all her living, has been also meekly deposited. The recent convert has brought his thanksgiving offering; and he rescued from the borders of the grave has added his memorial. The father whose prayers have been answered in the conversion of his children has laid his gift upon the altar, with the outpourings of a full heart; and he whose children have been snatched from the grave has linked them, by his benefactions, to the Bible cause. Many in pity for the destitute, and many from simple conviction of obligation, have cast in their gifts. The living have bestowed freely, and reaped the joy of the incoming harvest; while others have provided for an effective remembrance of their love for the Bible and deep interest in the perishing when they have been gathered to their rest, and may watch at the heavenly portals for the coming converts. Large benefactions have come; so have many a thousand-multiplied farthings of the little ones. The illustrations have been beautiful and constant of what Dr. Chalmers designated "the power of littles." I shall never forget the emphatic statement of Mr. John L. Nitchie, long the General Agent, made many years ago at a Bible Anniversary we attended by appointment, that "our Bible work is sustained by the sixpences and the shillings." Our auxiliaries see this constantly. The flowing in of these streams—these many, many streams—has done for us wonderful things. Let us look at the footings presented by decades:

1st year	1816-17	$37,779 35	11th year	1826-27	$60,194 13
2d "	1817-18	36,564 30	12th "	1827-28	75,879 93
3d "	1818-19	53,223 94	13th "	1828-29	101,426 72
4th "	1819-20	41,361 97	14th "	1829-30	143,449 81
5th "	1820-21	47,009 20	15th "	1830-31	116,900 74
6th "	1821-22	40,082 34	16th "	1831-32	86,875 18
7th "	1822-23	52,021 75	17th "	1832-33	83,556 03
8th "	1823-24	42,416 95	18th "	1833-34	86,537 63
9th "	1824-25	44,833 08	19th "	1834-35	98,306 29
10th "	1825-26	53,039 85	20th "	1835-36	101,771 48
		$449,532 73			$951,897 94
21st year	1836-37	$83,259 79	31st year	1846-47	$203,494 63
22d "	1837-38	91,904 57	32d "	1847-48	251,804 68
23d "	1838-39	79,545 24	33d "	1848-49	236,428 94
24th "	1839-40	94,880 24	34th "	1849-50	284,459 59
25th "	1840-41	116,485 05	35th "	1850-51	276,882 53
26th "	1841-42	132,637 08	36th "	1851-52	308,744 81
27th "	1842-43	124,728 77	37th "	1852-53	346,542 42
28th "	1843-44	153,678 05	38th "	1853-54	394,340 50
29th "	1844-45	159,738 68	39th "	1854-55	346,767 09
30th "	1845-46	196,182 48	40th "	1855-56	393,167 25
		$1,233,039 95			$3,042,632 44
41st year	1856-57	$441,805 67	1st decade		$449,532 73
42d "	1857-58	390,759 49	2d "		951,897 94
43d "	1858-59	415,011 37	3d "		1,233,039 95
44th "	1859-60	435,956 92	4th "		3,042,632 44
45th "	1860-61	389,541 52	5th "		4,751,850 08
46th "	1861-62	378,132 08			
47th "	1862-63	422,588 00	Total,		$10,434,953 74
48th "	1863-64	560,578 60			
49th "	1864-65	677,851 39			
50th "	1865-66	642,625 64			
		$4,751,850 08			

Here you see the agency which has set up the printing press, multiplied our electrotype plates, and has sent out millions of volumes on a life giving errand. Can this be lost? Ah, it is all committed to the gracious One, who has moved the hearts of the people, and who has said, "My word shall not return unto me void, but it shall accomplish that whereto I sent it."

5. *The Christian countenance and co-operation* enjoyed is to be mentioned as one of the special sources of animating power. How trying and how painful is it to work alone! How the heart sinks when without sympathy, without a word of good cheer! How hard has it been found to persevere, even in a right and good cause, without some favouring on-looker and ally! This has not been our case. Opposition there has been, and Bible burning there has been, by the blind followers and tools of antichrist. Infidelity has sneered or amused itself with our Bible fanaticism, as it would call it. But from a cloud of witnesses, of men honoured and revered in the records of the good, the great, the talented, and the useful, have come the words of good cheer. Ours have been a John Quincy Adams, a Richard Varick, a De Witt Clinton, a Chancellor Kent, a Judge M'Lean, a Bayard, a Van Rensselaer, a Murray, an Irving, a Butler, a Woodworth, and a galaxy of others, who on our public occasions have borne strong and animating testimony in behalf of our great enterprise. Over our whole land the voices of representative men have given timely impetus to the work in the fields occupied by our auxiliaries. While the clergy might be expected to throw their influence into the Bible cause, which is in its turn their most efficient ally, and have been our warm and earnestly co-operating friends, from all the professions have come the same strong notes of encouragement. From the highest positions in the army and navy, from the professoral chairs in our colleges and universities, from the counting room and the shop, from the bench and the bar, from all classes and conditions, there has been but one strain—"Go forward; the work is of God." We are not an ecclesiastical organization, and propose in no way to mingle in ecclesiastical affairs as a society. Our prayer is for the prevalence of our common Christianity over the whole earth. Whatever may be our private

relations, our work here is of such a character, that we cannot but be affected by the approbation and commendation of the brethren of the denominations represented among us. We record it frankly, that we and our co-labourers are moved to greater effort by the favouring action of General Assemblies, Synods, Councils, Conventions, and Associations. We feel a greater confidence in our Cause; our hearts are bound more firmly together in its promotion; we tread more firmly over the path of difficulty; we rise above discouragements more easily, as the fathers and brethren are with us.

From abroad also has come to us the warm greeting and hearty Christian salutation. Our Board in its first Report recognises the fact, that the British and Foreign Bible Society first called attention to the importance of an American National Society. When it was organized, their early gifts were most opportune, and their cordial expressions of satisfaction in our expanding operations have been uniform and often repeated. In the time of our civil strife, apprehending some pressure on our means of usefulness and the possible curtailment of plans, they generously proffered a liberal pecuniary gift. Their kind countenance has combined with their liberality in brightening and strengthening the golden links of union. Co-labourers on the continental field echo the Jubilee song and bid us "God speed." All this and such as this along our entire pathway, how can it but exhilarate, and give new energy, and call out greater effort?

6. *Our Agents* through the country have claims on our notice, in this connexion, of no ordinary character, as they have been eminently an arm of power, and vigilant watchers over Bible interests every where. The questions have been earnestly discussed in various directions, whether agents were not instruments who could be dispensed with, costing more than they were worth—mere sinecures. It is true, any good plan may be abused; an agent may be a burden instead of a blessing, and there may be an unwarrantable multiplication of them; and of course, then, the money paid them is wasted. So there may be cases where they are not needed, other instruments and motive powers being properly within reach, as is the case in strictly

denominational societies and boards. But with all deference we say, in the general benevolent organizations they are necessary. In such cases, there is nothing like the denomination tie to employ. Every thing is on the broad ground of usefulness and taking men as they are, and not as they should be, which we must do. No general cause can flourish without carefully selected agents. There is great force in the adage we have heard from childhood, "What is everybody's business is nobody's." The wise and right minded, earnest Agent is the arm of a society, felt at the most distant parts of a field; he is a constantly acting spring; he is a living mnemonic to faulty memories; a moral express, conveying the last intelligence concerning want and work; he is the substitute for many good men, who are so pressed with other matters, yet loving the good Cause, that they are ready to give their means when they cannot give their time; he is the ally of the pastor; his office is the opposite of a sinecure; he holds all the social and domestic ties, with all their tendernesses, at bay for his work's sake. In many a section of our country, in the transition from the wilderness state, he goes with his life in his hand. The societies never pamper him; and hence he is, in effect, not unfrequently the largest contributor to a good cause; for he sustains it by the greatest sacrifices.

Our Society has had and still has its Agents. The system grew up under the necessities of the case, and it has thrived through their services. Take them away, and the good Cause would immediately languish, and the rapidity of the decline would be in proportion as its parts were distant from the centre of interest and of activity. It must be said, and it is said with confidence, concerning our Agents as a body (for it is only as such that we can on this occasion speak of them), they have done a great and good work; they have built up the Bible cause in many a place, where previously not a movement had been made; they have kept alive interest and effort when they began to decline; they have revived societies which seemed ready to die. Theirs it has been to investigate wants and bring home appeals which have brought out the needed supplies. The plan on which our agency department is organized is very simple; is guarded at all points; is economical; is effective. We owe it, morally, every thing. Let us look at one month's report; for a faithful record of work done is kept, and has been from the beginning. Let us take the stormy month of February as our specimen:

During the month of February, reports were received from thirty of the Agents of this Society, and the following are the results of their labours: Agents reporting, 30; auxiliaries and committees visited, 111; meetings held, 191; anniversaries attended, 46; auxiliaries and committees organized, 33; sermons and addresses delivered, 230; letters and circulars sent, 8,656; miles travelled, 12,562; amount of donations collected by the Agents, $7,797 65; amount received by them from the sale of books, $4,061 06; amount remitted by them to the Parent Society, $17,021 31; amount paid by them into the treasuries of auxiliaries, $2,465 78; amount of subscriptions secured, $2,092 95; number of families visited in their fields, 24,001; number of destitute families found, 1,046; number of destitute families supplied, 810; number of destitute individuals supplied, 115; Sabbath schools supplied, 41; volumes circulated by sale, 3,349; by donation, 2,068; value of volumes sold, $3,687 70; donated, $1,065 64. Total receipts from sales and donations, $14,192 78.

7. To the Board of Managers we give a *special place* in this enumeration.

The provision of the Constitution is: "A Board of Managers shall be appointed to conduct the business of the Society, consisting of thirty-six laymen," etc. With these, various clergymen are associated in most of the Standing Committees, the Constitution giving ministers who are life members "the same power as the Manager himself."

The clerical representation in the Committees of the Board has been taken from all the denominations participating in the Society, and has been composed of the most active and influential men. Their time and attention and co-operation have been most cheerfully given, and their wisdom has aided much in shaping the business of the Board, and giving life and energy to the whole working of the Institution. The speaker may say of his brethren, that in the whole onward progress of the Society, they have constituted an indispensable agency for good.

The Lay Managers can scarcely be presented too strongly in a fair account of the instruments which have built up the National Bible Society. One who has been in the midst of them for years, and has known many of them personally, and attended their deliberations often through a range of some thirty years, may speak of what he knows and has seen. They will excuse me for saying what I deem due without asking their permission, and of course, without previous knowledge of my purpose.

The Society was very happy in the selections of its first Board, as all will say who knew the men. They were men of practical wisdom; loving the Cause for its own sake. Intelligent, able, of known integrity, and selected for the service and having the confidence of all. They did a good work in carrying the infant institution through its weak state and all its attendant perils, to a condition of maturity and of strength. They have gone to their rest and their reward, not one remaining to be present with us this Jubilee. But they bequeathed their precious charge to worthy hands. In the construction of the Board of Managers, there has always been the wisdom of age mingling with the earnestness of vigorous manhood; they have been men of various professions, pursuits, and conditions, acquainted with the world, understanding thoroughly the complications of business, intrusted with other interests of high moment, men of principle, of character, of piety, placed in committees for which their pursuits fitted them. They have been charged with heavy responsibilities—most momentous issues were pended on their deliberations—their hall of meeting has been a Senate Chamber.

The business of the Society very early developed itself in such forms as to require modifications of the first plans, and there was necessarily a division of labour. The Committees are as follows, viz.: on Publication, on Finance, on Distribution, on Agencies, on Anniversaries, on Versions, on Legacies, an Auditing Committee, and one on Nominations.

By the plan adopted, every subject to be acted on passes through the careful examination of its appropriate Committee, and is then brought before the whole Board, and is again considered fully, if deemed necessary, and passed upon. When difficult and delicate questions are to be considered, they are examined by larger committees, and by them recommended to the Board or disapproved. Calmness, thoroughness, impartiality, intelligence, courtesy reign. In the Committee, whose meetings are monthly, and oftener when required, the same fidelity has reigned, and hours have been necessary to do the work.

For this work all the affairs of a man's own business were laid by for the time—it was felt to be a solemn while it was regarded as a pleasant duty thus to be engaged. Thus, men have been occupied year after year, and the grand consideration has been, to be useful in the cause of the Bible and of humanity, and to voluntary services they have liberally added of their means to the Bible Treasury. They have been and are the main spring of action, while they are ever watchful guardians and conservators of right action. Without such a Board of Managers, so constituted, so animated, the great work never could have reached its present magnificent dimensions. They are the men under God who have made us what we are as an Institution. I beg they will pardon me while I say, Noble men! you are the benefactors of millions; we honour your principles and your practice in this behalf: we ask for you the richest of blessings.

8. *The Presiding and Executive auspices*, under which our onward course has been pursued, claim a special notice at this point, may I not say, a crowning place in my narrative?

How much depends on having a proper head—how much on having a presiding mind—clear, well balanced, intelligent, decided, and yet complaisant, possessed of sharp discriminations, a breadth of view equal to the actual field of labour, and a justness of estimation of both difficulties and encouragements and of the means of adaptation to each; such a head a great enterprise demands.

It is matter of grateful note, that God both raises up men and fits them for exigencies. This was eminently verified in the organization of this Society, the men who were active in the work being the men for the time and for the great enterprise to be undertaken. Their high character gave interest and tone to the movement. All this was especially true of the men who have successively presided over and occupied executive places in the Board.

All eyes and hearts were turned to Elias Boudinot as the

first President, and he brought to the office a mind well stored with various attainments—an eminently matured character—a reputation, acquired in offices of high trust and responsibility interwoven with our country's most critical period, without a stain, and as wide as our country, and a depth and warmth of piety which was as characteristic as his integrity and intelligence. Trained to the law, admitted to and presiding over Congress in the final act which gave peace and an acknowledged separate nationality to our country, and, having served his country well, he gave the mellowness of his life to the direct promotion of the spiritual interests of his fellow men. He had already been long in the fellowship of the First Presbyterian Church of Elizabeth, N. J., and for many years an active Trustee, and at twenty-five years of age made its Treasurer.

On retiring from civil life, he took up his residence at Burlington, N. J. "His heart expanding with the noblest principles of Christian benevolence, he contributed liberally to institutions whose objects were the extension of literature and religion, and his name is cherished among them as a munificent benefactor." In his relation as President of the New Jersey Bible Society (organized in 1809), he had seen the efficiency of united effort, and longed and laboured most earnestly to see one grand central movement, which should combine all the separate organizations in the country. The organization of the American Bible Society was one of the happiest events of his life. When he was chosen to be its first President, he felt that he had received the highest honour of an honoured life.

His liberal donations to the Society when in its weakness placed it on a firm foundation. It has been well said: "This splendid moral structure, the monument of the Protestant Christianity of the nation, is also in a special sense his monument. A nobler one no man can have." Distinguished as a philanthropist, a scholar, a patriot, and a Christian, he passed to his heavenly rest, after a pilgrimage of fourscore and one years.

The venerable Chief Justice, John Jay, the First Vice President, succeeded to the Presidency, and it may be truly said, his name was a tower of strength. He was devoted to his country, but even more devoted to the cause of Christ. It was in the time which tried men's souls that he entered upon public life, and though not mingling in the conflicts of the field, he won renown in the equally important field of Congressional action, where he became the presiding mind, and with a noble band gave form and shape to its deliberations and acts. Wise in counsel, clear, sound, discriminating, among the most accomplished civilians of his time, he was the man to represent his country abroad at any of the courts of Europe, and take an active, yes, a leading part in the most delicate missions. A native New Yorker, he had at heart the interests of this commonwealth, and sought her welfare and gave the form of her first Constitution, whose principles it were well if now in many respects possessed. Descended from the persecuted Huguenots, as was Boudinot, he drank in the spirit of liberty and a free Christianity with his earliest breath. Having served his country well, he retired to the quietness and simple charms of rural life at Bedford, Westchester County, N. Y., and to religious culture in the bosom of the Protestant Episcopal Church. We cannot but think of him as the Christian Sage, as in his retirement he gave himself to the study of God's Holy Word, which had been his "songs in the house of his pilgrimage," and in his golden evening of a varied life was his chief comfort and joy. His infirm state of health prevented his attendance at the anniversaries, but his addresses sent from his Patmos (I had almost said), full of love, breathing the true Christian spirit, ministering the soundest counsel, were inspiriting. There was a moral power in his character which gave power to his words.

The year of his resignation, in consequence of his advanced age, was one of solemn monition and bereavement to the Bible cause. Vice Presidents Tilghman, Worthington, Phillips, and DeWitt Clinton, whose great influence was given to the Cause, were gathered to their fathers. Had the last survived, he would probably have succeeded Mr. Jay in the chair which he occupied with dignity and eloquence at the Anniversary of 1827.

But the same Providence which gave the first and second Presidents gave us Richard Varick as the third, who had been our first Treasurer and the first President of the New York Sunday School Union, one of the most honoured and honourable men of our day. It deserves our special notice, that our first three Presidents were heroes of the Revolution—one in civil life, two in connexion with the army, and one of these (the last) a participant in the hard service of the battle field. It is true then that the distinguished soldier may be also the distinguished Christian.

Colonel Varick was of Holland descent, a stock which knew the horrors of persecution for conscience' sake, and learnt in the death of an army of martyrs, as the Huguenots did, the value of a free Gospel and an open Bible. Colonel Varick early entered the army as Captain of the First New York, and was advanced rapidly to positions of responsibility, and became and continued for years a most beloved member of Washington's military family. He was a man of great dignity of person, with great kindness of manner, of marked business and executive ability, of large heart, of firm purpose, of the sternest integrity, of strong and controlling love for the cause of piety and of all good men. He gave the whole weight of his social position, of his character, of his liberality, and of his piety, to the advancement of the Bible cause. He died in the occupancy of his office in his seventy-ninth year.

The distinguished John Cotton Smith, of Connecticut, of direct Puritan descent, one of the Vice Presidents from the organization of the Society (the first President of the Connecticut Bible Society, formed in 1809), was chosen as the fourth President of the American Bible Society. His position was among the first men of the land. Esteemed one of the most accomplished gentlemen in the performance of his various public trusts as a judge, a Congressional representative, a State executive, he crowned all with eminent piety. The year 1810 witnessed the organization of the American Board of Commissioners for Foreign Missions, an institution whose blessed influence has been felt over all lands, and is destined to be recognised as the most efficient agency in our land in bringing on "the latter day glory." In its success, Governor Smith felt the greatest interest. In 1823 he became its Vice President, and in 1826 its President, and continued such till 1841. He occupied for many years, with winning grace of manner, the two positions of President of two of the most important institutions of the day. It was his privilege to see both rise from small beginnings to great strength, and the promise opening to both of a most successful future. During thirty years connexion with Bible work, he had seen those whose place was beside him in office pass away, and of the thirty-six Managers, only a few remaining. He was spared to see fourscore years and one, and to enjoy all the supports and consolations of religion in his declining days. His memory is tenderly cherished.

It was a kind Providence who gave us in April, 1846, as our next President, the Hon. Theodore Frelinghuysen, then Chancellor of the University of the City of New York. Few men have so widely and so tenderly endeared themselves to every circle with which connected as did he. Gifted with a most kindly and generous temperament—intelligent, frank, confiding and pure in all his principles, the friend of all; it seemed as if all were his friends. Bred a lawyer, he rose to the first rank in his profession in his native State, New Jersey, and representing her in the Senate of the United States when it embraced a large proportion of the greatest men our country has produced, he won the highest respect for his devotion to noble causes and his marked Christian character. It was his delight to be actively engaged in doing good to his fellow men, and accordingly, all the great institutions of the day received his warm support, while his Sabbaths were given to the Bible class. It was a suitable testimony to his character and his executive ability, that he was for sixteen years President of the American Board of Commissioners for Foreign Missions, succeeding Governor Smith; for six years (from 1842 to 1848) President of the American Tract Society, and for sixteen years President of the American Bible Society, and as such, closed his earthly career. For forty-five years he had illustrated the excellence of the Gospel, in a harmonious and beautiful Christian life, and enjoyed at its close perfect peace.

His name and character are familiar and dear in all the churches of our land, and his removal was felt to be a great public loss.

The Hon. Luther Bradish, connected with the Episcopal Church, one of the Vice Presidents, was chosen to fill the vacancy in 1862. During several years after his predecessor had removed to New Brunswick, to become the President of Rutgers College, he presided at the monthly meetings of the Board, and proved himself an admirable Chairman; indeed, of all the Presidents he would be called the great parliamentarian. He gave himself most earnestly and devotedly to the business of the Society, and by a most happy combination of dignity and urbanity gave interest to all our meetings, and secured great despatch in our business.

Less known among the churches generally than his predecessors, he was, where known, esteemed a truly Christian man; liberal in his views and loving all good men, and freely mingling in the interchange of Christian courtesies. In his political career and in charge of high civil trusts, as a legislator and citizen, he won the confidence of all. He has left his mark in the various business interests of the Board.

He was not spared to us long as our presiding officer. In 1863, in the monthly meeting of the Board in August, he performed his last public service, and left us to close his life at Newport, R. I., at eighty years of age.

"It is a striking fact, in the lives of the Presidents of the American Bible Society, that they all reached such advanced ages with dignity and usefulness. Boudinot died aged eighty-one years; Jay, eighty-four; Varick, seventy-eight; Smith, eighty-one; Frelinghuysen, seventy-five; Bradish, eighty;" all of them men of mark.

But not these alone are to be regarded as our commendations to lovers of Bible diffusion—their moral excellence being part of our capital. Close to them are to be placed the distinguished Secretaries, who have been the pilots of our richly freighted craft through its onward course. The following have served in that office, viz.: Rev. J. M. Mason, D.D.; Rev. J. B. Romeyn, D.D.; John Pintard, LL.D.; Rev. James Milner, D.D.; Rev. S. S. Woodhull, D.D.; Rev. Thomas M'Auley, D.D., LL.D.; Rev. Charles G. Somers; Rev. Nathan Bangs, D.D.; Rev. John C. Brigham, D.D.; Robert F. Winslow, Esq.; Rev. Spencer H. Cone, D.D.; Rev. Edmund S. Janes, D.D.; Rev. Noah Levings, D.D.; Rev. S. Ireneus Prime, D.D.; Rev.

Joseph Holdich, D.D.; Rev. Joseph C. Stiles, D.D.; Rev. James H. M'Neill; and Rev. Wm. J. R. Taylor, D.D.*

The earliest performed their work without compensation, being pastors at the same time, but soon it was found that the proper accomplishment of the rapidly growing work demanded the entire time of the Secretaries, and that they must be sustained by the Society. Circumstances required also that the number should be increased, and this was but the evidence of the Society's prosperity. It is not praise, but the simple statement of fact to say, they were strong men. The churches to which they were attached gave them their high position before they came to us, and what they had and what they were was given to our service. They have pleaded our Cause through the land; they have kept a vigilant eye over all our interests at home and abroad; they have been our medium of connexion with all the actors and co-operators in our work; they have cheered the disheartened, they have revived the declining; they have mapped out the field of work for all; they have been always ready, always pressing on, and in a sense, carrying us with them. The documents prepared by them, the appeals and addresses made by them, diffused every where, the various guides and manuals written by them for every branch of service, the constant work with all the Committees, their vast correspondence, their quarterly extracts, their monthly records of the progress of the Cause, so many monthly telegrams sent through our Bible connexions, constitute a great body of Bible Society literature. Some of them have gone to their reward in the Master's presence, others have gone to other departments of Christian labour and responsibility where blessings attend them.† Theirs has been ever a great lever power.

IV. And now, standing on the verge of the half century, what are our *Prospects?*

We have reached a point of intelligent observation. With all our experiences, our tests of principles, our success in overcoming difficulties, our knowledge of our reliances, our multi-

* Since the Sermon was preached, Rev. T. Ralston Smith has been chosen Secretary.

† See Appendix (E.)

plied appliances, we are qualified to make estimates for the future.

To the inquiry, What are our prospects, what is before us? The outlook gives a definite, clear answer; it is that there is work to be done—a great work, a glorious work, to be done. Let not any be startled at this announcement. It is to be regarded as a privilege, as a blessing, that there is work for us all to do. Our Christian benefactions furnish the best training school for all the better feelings of the heart, while they bring to us a present sweet reward. Alas for us when the Master has no more work for us. It will be the omen of a denial by Him; it will be the keenest rebuke to our past unfaithfulness if He refuse us a place among his workers. What a thought it would be that He has no further use for us!

In this department of Christian labour, work can never be said to be done. The missionary may reach a point where he may be able to retire from his labour in a given section, as he may have seen his work crowned with such a succession of blessings, that he may commit it to native Christians and native preachers and pastors. Not so with us; paradoxical as it may be, our work is always done and always yet to be done; that is, while we satisfy present calls, others will constantly rise and press us. Populations with us are constantly changing, not only in the natural course of generation coming after generation in the same region, but by the flowing out of multitudes over, what is at a given time, new territory. Thus new fields are constantly in preparation for Bible work, and this tide of outflow through the discovery of new mineral lands is destined to be greatly increased.

It is but a decade of years since the older portions of our land were by one grand movement supplied, and yet from the whole range of the Northern and Eastern and Northwestern States, the intelligence meets us of the necessity of repeating the process. Where it would be little thought true, the number of families without the Sacred Scriptures is painfully large. It seems that the statements which years since stirred every heart may be repeated to the letter, and be true. We cannot wonder at this; new multitudes have grown to maturity and entered on family responsibilities; accessions have come in largely from other lands, and calls for these are independent of the loss of the Sacred Volume by carelessness, by wear and tear, and by calamity. All this relates to a portion of the land where the direct conflicts and ravages of war have not come.

What must be the wants where war, always horrible, even when just, has trodden with iron hoof and crushing power! Every traveller, every returning tourist fills our hearts with sorrow and awakens our sympathy by the account of fortunes gone; poverty and consequent distress reigning, sanctuaries burned, homes desolated. In all this, how fares the Bible? However prized, can it alone be saved? No; it goes in the common ruin. Look every where over the Southern country, and you see fields inviting most earnest labour, and hearts longing for it and thankful for it. And this is the most uniting work we can do. The Politician and the Statesman are busy with the discussion of modes of reconstruction, and we are all interested in it; but here we have the means of winning hearts and annealing the broken parts in love; it is a Christian reconstruction—not less valuable and effective, because it is unostentatious and without the flourish of trumpets.

War has broken down every barrier and given us access to millions to whom this Sacred Word is the most precious of boons. The millions of Freedmen, made such by the results of war, stretch out to us their imploring hands. Their need is urgent in proportion to their former condition. Many had access to a degree of religious privileges, but the great mass were in darkness. Now, the way is fully open to do them good, and by Christian processes fit them for the Divine will concerning them. We look forward with hope concerning them; but that hope is interwoven with the fidelity of those who may bless them with the means of Christian improvement and elevation.

Our Board at its recent meeting, the closing one of the Jubilee year, declared its policy as to the new half century; it comprehends the full occupation and cultivation of the American field. What a glorious work it will be!*

But this is not all. We cannot intermit; no, we must in-

* See Appendix (F.)

crease, if possible, a hundredfold our work abroad. What has been done seems but the beginning; it is but a mere impression on the sad conditions of the pagan world. The millions we speak of on our own continent are a mere fraction of needy humanity in comparison with the hundreds of millions who have no message of mercy, who have no Word of Life. The mind is overwhelmed and the heart bleeds as we dwell on the details furnished by the faithful missionary, the herald of their wants.

To these millions we are most solemnly bound by the pledges of the past. We cannot withdraw our hand from the undertakings now in their infancy. We stand committed to the Christian labourers now at the various outposts of Christian civilization, and along the frontier line committed to Christianity, committed to us by God. But there is no thought of drawing back—if there were, the shades of our fathers in the Bible work would rebuke us as unfaithful stewards in charge of the highest of trusts. The keen rebuke, mingled with pity, would come to us from a thousand associated Christian labourers in other lands, who have followed our onward course with admiring love, and who send us their hearty greeting at our Jubilee.

Here then is work—most blessed work. One of old wept because he had no more worlds to conquer; but ours are to be tears, because they are so many parts of this vast world, after a work of fifty years, which are still unblest with the Word of Life; so many worlds of differing peoples for the truth yet to conquer.

But here is nothing to discourage or lead us to falter a moment. We are in *a condition* to do a greater work than ever. Our facilities are many and are admirable. The manner in which the pressure of the last five years has been met satisfies every one that our capabilities are equal to any emergency which in almost any circumstances can occur. Divine Providence has fostered us and cherished us into such a degree of strength, that we may be ready to respond to any call. This has been his design in all He has done.

The fathers in the Bible work had, as they thought, large views; and so they had. But scarcely one probably took into his earnest anticipation what has been done. More than ever is there force in the maxim: "Expect great things; attempt great things." We as the simple, natural employment of our internal power cannot say what may not be done in coming years.

Add to our facilities *our hearty co-labourers*, and what encouragement comes from this view. There is no doubt or uncertainty here. It is simply a question of common fidelity, not of utmost ability. We are told of 5,232 Bible societies and associations linked in common loving bonds in our Cause. What an army of giving, praying hearts is here. If these do their duty, is not here the arm of all moving power? What is too great a work for our National Society with such a reliance? Yes, and this co-operating army is not limited by the present; instead of the fathers come up the children, born to this work. But above all, who does not see that this is *God's work* which is before us, a work for the good of men; but above all, a work for his glory? May we not ask and look for his blessing? His past kindness sheds a heavenly radiance over the future. It puts into our lips the inquiry, Is any thing too hard for God? Is then any thing too rich for Him to dispense, any thing too rich to diffuse over the vast field from which he is gathering the thronging family of the Redeemer? He has said, "Open thy mouth wide, and I will fill it." He has not brought this Christian enterprise so far to forsake it.

My Brethren, ours have been contemplations of a peaceful work, but we should take into our account, that we have enemies to encounter in the conflict in which the Word, "the sword of the Spirit," is the only reliance.

There stands before us antichrist, grim, hoary, sending out his emissaries as of old, breathing the same spirit and ready to imbrue his hands in blood (were he not withheld by the conventionalities of a Christian civilization), as the bloody scenes at Barletta in Italy, under the fierce denouncements of ecclesiastical firebrands, brought to us within a few weeks, attest.

It is generally believed that a trial of strength of Protestant Christianity with Romanism is to be one of the great events of the age, and that the encroachments of Romanism and its aim at consolidation in our own country tend to hasten it. Let it be so; only let the Word of God go forth to the people; let it go unshackled, and the result will be glorious for a pure evangelism. Popery has never been able to stand before an open, free Bible. Hence the studied efforts and the exercise of a ghostly authority to keep the Word of God from the people, and the hostility to hear it merely read in the schools.

Some are startled by the increase of Romanists in our land; they need not be, for it can be readily accounted for by reference to accessions by emigration and by natural increase. The gain from Protestantism, though displayed with a flourish, is insignificant as a whole, and limited mostly to pupils in Papal schools and various educational houses, while on the other hand, the Bible has won multitudes to the true Gospel of our Lord Jesus Christ, whom no society record has published to the world. In this conflict of truth with error, "the weapons of our warfare are not carnal," no civil enactment is asked, no pains and penalties, but simply to let the Word go free and the individual conscience to be unshackled. We see then what in the coming years must be the work of every Bible society, and of every member of the evangelical churches in our land.

But the enemy seeks to carry his unhallowed end under the garb of science, and even in official religious robes to pare away the carved work of the Temple of Revelation, and undermine its claim to Divine origin. Solemn obligations and subscriptions are violated in the effort, and the common considerations which bind men are disregarded. Let infidelity, in whatever garb, do its work; only send the simple Word of Truth abroad, and it will hold its own and prevail. The Bible is its own witness; its amazing adaptations bring it very near to the hearts of a sorrowing, sin-stricken race. There is about it, and in it and its accessories, that which impresses the mind with the idea of its divinity.

If these two forms of opposition are to contest the control of the mind of the coming generations, the course of duty is made very plain and urgent; it is, to place the Bible in whole or in part in every man's hand, and we need not a prophet to tell the result. The past has made the record. The Word of Life has been attacked by keen minds; it has encountered fierce opposition in every age, and now, though the mode of attack has assumed new forms, the Rock will be found immoveable; only let those who love the Bible do their duty. The God of the Bible is with his own Word.

My Brethren:—From the morning of Thursday next, we enter upon a new epoch in the history of our National Bible Institution, and in the most favourable circumstances, with every thing to encourage and call out energy. A solemn, touching scene occurred at the closing meeting of the Board's work on Thursday last. There stood a venerable surviving clerical member of the convention which formed the Society (one of the last two), Dr. Gardiner Spring. There were gathered about him many impressing circumstances; advanced far on in his journey to the better land, a most faithful friend of the Cause—infirm, his heart overflowing with Christian love, standing where he had often stood, in tender tone he told us of those who were gone with whom he had laboured; he uttered himself as feeling as if this were his last meeting with the Board; it was the *half century just ending, giving its last counsel to the half century just entering;* its plea was for the work to be done. Touching, solemn appeal! shall not we hear it whose heads blossom with the evidences of threescore years? Shall not the mature and vigorous hear it? Shall not they just putting on the harness of labour hear it? Before God are we not ready to say, We hear it, we will heed it? In a few days the Jubilee call will gather in solemn meeting a great assemblage of friends and co-labourers, who will come from the North and the South, from the East and the West, to bear their gladsome testimony to the kindness and abounding blessing of the God of the Bible, and shall it not be also for solemn consecration to the work now so widely inviting our efforts? God grant it may be so, and add his crowning blessing,* and

To Him shall be all the Glory.

* See Appendix (G.)

APPENDIX.

(A) Samuel J. Mills was a remarkable man, and was made in the providence of God a most honoured instrument in the advancement of the Redeemer's kingdom, and thereby blessing his fellow men. He was born in 1783 of pious parents (his father being a clergyman), at Torringford, in Connecticut. He enjoyed the faithful instruction and pious care of his excellent parents for some sixteen years, when he left home for the purposes of education. In his fifteenth year, he was awakened to a proper consideration of his condition as a sinner in the time of a wide spread revival, and for two years was the subject of a most unhappy state of mind. When he "found peace in believing" and "rejoiced in hope of the glory of God," his feeling, as expressed to his father, was, "that he could not conceive of any course of life in which to pass the rest of his days, that was so pleasant as to go and communicate the Gospel salvation to the poor heathen;" and this was in harmony with his pious mother's aim concerning him from his birth. From that hour, his whole life had one direction, as was shown in his studies, his associations, his reading, his labours. God honoured him early as an instrument of good to his fellow men, as when in college a precious visitation of mercy was granted in connexion with his Christian faithfulness and prayers. He soon unbosomed himself to his fellow students, who became distinguished missionaries afterwards: Gordon Hall and James Richards, for many years in India. Soon others joined the little group, and by the hay stack, in a meadow near Williams College, in prayer and fasting, they prepared for their life work. The result in Divine providence was, the formation of a society of Inquiry in their own college, and similar societies in other colleges and in theological seminaries, and at length, the formal, solemn offer of themselves to be sent to the heathen, by the General Association of Massachusetts Proper, in June, 1810. Very soon this was followed by the formation of the American Board, and a goodly company, influenced largely by the earnest appeals of Mr. Mills, embarked under its auspices for the highest work of the Church, bearing the Gospel of salvation to the perishing.

After his licensure, Mr. Mills mingled largely with Christian men, clergymen, and laymen, in every proper form, and with earnest, winning, and simple manner urging on various forms of Christian effort. Dr. Griffin, President of Williams College, said: "I have been in situations to *know*, that from the counsels formed in that sacred conclave (referring to the meetings of Mills and his little company for prayer and conference), or from the mind of Mills himself, arose the American Board of Commissioners for Foreign Missions, the American Bible Society, the United Foreign Missionary Society, and the African School, under the care of the Synod of New York and New Jersey, besides all the impetus given to the Domestic Missions, to the Colonization Society, and to the general cause of benevolence in both hemispheres." He then adds: "If I had any instrumentality in originating any of these measures, I here publicly declare, that in every instance I received the first impulse from Samuel John Mills."

To the interests of Africa he gave himself finally. On the 16th of November, 1817, he left his home as an Agent of the American Colonization Society, and when arrived at his field of labour, he was occupied with unwearied efforts in the way of frequent and protracted conferences with the native kings along the coast to accomplish his object—that of opening a way for the settlement of coloured emigrants from this country.

It was his last work. Having fully prepared the way for the Colonization Society, he left Sierra Leone on his return voyage; was taken ill while at sea, and after a conflict of nearly a fortnight with disease, he was called home. He gently closed his hands on his breast as if to engage in some act of devotion, and while a celestial smile settled upon his countenance, and every feature expressed the serenity and meekness of his soul, he ceased to breathe. "No monumental marble records his worth;" his monuments are the great and blessed agencies he was so largely instrumental in organizing, and while they live, his memory lives.

(B) MEMBERS OF THE CONVENTION

WHO FORMED THE AMERICAN BIBLE SOCIETY: CONSTITUTED, BY THE BOARD OF MANAGERS, DIRECTORS FOR LIFE.

Basset, Rev. John, D.D., Bushwick, Long Island, N. Y.
Bayard, Samuel, Princeton, N. J.
Beecher, Rev. Lyman, D.D., *Secretary of the Convention*, Cincinnati, Ohio.
Biggs, Rev. Thomas J., Cincinnati, Ohio.
Blatchford, Rev. Samuel, D.D., Lansingburgh, N. Y.
Blythe, Rev. James, D.D., South Hanover, Indiana.
Bogart, Rev. David S., New York.
Bradford, Rev. John M., D.D., Albany, N. Y.
Burd, William, St. Louis, Missouri.
Caldwell, John E., New York.
Callender, Levi, Greenville, N. Y.
Chester, Rev. John, D.D., Albany, N. Y.
Clarke, Matthew St. Clair, Washington, D. C.
Cooley, Rev. Eli F., Monmouth, N. J.
Cooper, James Fennimore, New York.
Day, Orrin, Catskill, N. Y.
Eddy, Thomas, New York.
Ford, Rev. Henry, Elmira, N. Y.
Forrest, Rev. Robert, Roseville, N. Y.
Griscom, John, LL.D., Trenton, N. J.
Hall, Rev. James, D.D., Statesville, N. C.
Henshaw, Rt. Rev. J. P. K., D.D., Providence, R. I.
Hornblower, Joseph C., LL.D., Newark, N. J., Vice President.
Humphrey, Rev. Heman, D.D., Pittsfield, Mass.
Jay, William, Bedford, N. Y., Vice President.
Jones, Rev. David, Holmesburgh, Pa.
Lewis, Rev. Isaac, D.D., Greenwich, Ct.
Linklaen, Gen. John, Cazenovia, N. Y.
M'Dowell, Rev. John, D.D., Philadelphia, Pa.
Mason, Rev. John M., D.D., New York.
Milledoler, Rev. Philip, D.D., New York.
Morse, Rev. Jedediah, D.D., New Haven, Ct.
Mott, Valentine, M.D., New York.
Mulligan, William C., New York.
Murray, John, Jr., New York.
Neil, Rev. William, D.D., Philadelphia, Pa.
Nott, Rev. Eliphalet, D.D., Schenectady, N. Y.
Oliver, Rev. Andrew, Springfield, N. Y.
Platt, Rev. Isaac W., Athens, Pa.
Proudfit, Rev. Alexander, D.D., New York.
Rice, Rev. John H., D.D., Virginia.
Richards, Rev. Jas., D.D., Auburn, N. Y.
Romeyn, Rev. John B., D.D., *Secretary of the Convention*, New York.
Sands, Joshua, Brooklyn, N. Y.
Sayres, Rev. Gilbert H., Jamaica, N. Y.
Sedgwick, Robert, New York.
Skinner, Ichabod, Washington, D. C.
Spring, Rev. S., D.D., Newburyport, Massachusetts.
Spring, Rev. Gardiner, D.D., New York.
Swift, Gen. Joseph G., Brooklyn, N. Y.
Taylor, Rev. N. W., D.D., New Haven, Ct.
Van Sinderen, Adrian, Brooklyn, N. Y.
Vroom, Guysbert B., New York.
Wallace, Joshua M., *President of the Convention*, Burlington, N. J.
Warner, Henry W., New York.
Williams, Rev. John, New York.
Williams, William, Vernon, N. Y.
Wilmur, Rev. Simon, Swedesboro', N. J.
Woodhull, Rev. George S., New Jersey.
Wright, Charles, Flushing, L. I., N. Y.

FIRST BOARD OF MANAGERS.

HENRY RUTGERS.
JOHN BINGHAM.
RICHARD VARICK.
THOMAS FARMAR.
STEPHEN VAN RENSSELAER.
SAMUEL BOYD.
GEORGE SUCKLEY.
DIVIE BETHUNE.
WILLIAM BAYARD.
PETER M'CARTEE.
THOMAS SHIELDS.
ROBERT RALSTON.
JOHN R. B. RODGERS.
DR. PETER WILSON.
JEREMIAH EVARTS.
JOHN WATTS, M.D.
THOMAS EDDY.
WILLIAM JOHNSON.
EBENEZER BURRILL.
ANDREW GIFFORD.
GEORGE GOSMAN.
THOMAS CARPENTER.
LEONARD BLEEKER.
JOHN CALDWELL.
RUFUS KING.
THOMAS STOKES.
JOSHUA SANDS.
GEORGE WARNER.
DE WITT CLINTON.
JOHN WARDER.
SAMUEL BAYARD.
DUNCAN P. CAMPBELL.
JOHN ASPINWALL.
JOHN MURRAY, JUN.
CHARLES WRIGHT.
CORNELIUS HEYER.

OFFICERS OF THE AMERICAN BIBLE SOCIETY.

President.

HON. ELIAS BOUDINOT, New Jersey.

Vice Presidents.

HON. JOHN JAY, New York.
MATTHEW CLARKSON, Esq., New York.
HON. SMITH THOMPSON, New York.
" JOHN LANGDON, New Hampshire.
" CALEB STRONG, Massachusetts.
" WILLIAM GRAY, Massachusetts.
" JOHN COTTON SMITH, Connecticut.
" JONAS GALUSHA, Vermont.
" WILLIAM JONES, Rhode Island.
" ISAAC SHELBY, Kentucky.
GEORGE MADISON, Esq., Kentucky.
HON. WILLIAM TILGHMAN, Pennsylvania.
" BUSHROD WASHINGTON, Virginia.
WILLIAM WIRT, Esq., Virginia.
HON. CHARLES C. PINCKNEY, South Carolina.
" WILLIAM GASTON, North Carolina.
" THOMAS WORTHINGTON, Ohio.
" THOMAS POSEY, Indiana.
" JAMES BROWN, Louisiana.
JOHN BOLTON, Esq., Georgia.
HON. FELIX GRUNDY, Tennessee.
ROBERT OLIVER, Esq., Maryland.
JOSEPH NOURSE, Esq., District of Columbia.

Secretary for Foreign Correspondence.

REV. DR. J. M. MASON.

Secretary for Domestic Correspondence.

REV. DR. J. B. ROMEYN.

Treasurer.

RICHARD VARICK, Esq.

(D) ARABIC SCRIPTURES.

THE ACTION OF THE BOARD OF MANAGERS.

The Board of Managers, at its regular meeting, on the third day of November, 1864, *unanimously adopted* the following report, which was first presented unanimously by a Committee consisting of the Standing Committees on Distribution, Publication, and Finance :—

Having heard all the correspondence in the hands of the Secretaries in reference to it, and had a free interchange of views, they are constrained to regard the electrotyping of the Arabic Version of the Scriptures by the Syrian Mission, as one of the most important undertakings which can claim the aid of the American Bible Society. The version, it appears, has been most carefully made, and by the most competent scholars on the field where it is first to be used; and has been approved by the Missionaries of various evangelical bodies represented therein. The statement made by the Mission in their last communication is worthy of note: "As touching the fidelity, excellence, and unsectarian character of the translation, it is important to notice that this has been the work of the *Mission*—not of an individual or individuals. It is not of yesterday, but has occupied *sixteen years* of almost consecutive labour in preparation and execution. The Mission set apart to it those who by endowment and by study seemed pre-eminently fitted for its prosecution."

The names of the translators—of Dr. Eli Smith, to whom it was given to lay the foundation of the work, and of Dr. Van Dyck, by whom it has been completed—are ample guarantee to all linguists conversant with the facts of the case, that both with respect to conformity to the original tongues and in rendering into Arabic, as excellent and faithful a translation has been secured as could be secured in any language. Besides these translators, chosen from their own number, the Mission has employed the best native talent that could be procured in the country to make the translation elegant as well as faithful, that it should conform to the native style of expression and to the highest standard of literary taste, and they believe that they have been peculiarly favoured in securing coadjutors of so high repute from both Christian and Mohammedan scholars. A still further guarantee to the fidelity of the translation, and one which applies also to its unsectarian character, is that each sheet of the translation, before being finally printed, was submitted to the careful scrutiny of all the members of the Mission; to interested native scholars of all sects; to other American Missionaries besides themselves; to English, German, Scotch, and Irish Missionaries of different religious denominations and in different parts of this empire (these proof-sheets being about thirty in number); that criticism has been freely invited and courted, has been offered and duly weighed, and from all these quarters have come warm and unqualified expressions of approbation and confidence.

The field to which this version is adapted is vast, embracing the Arabic-speaking population, extending from the Straits of Gibraltar to Peking, from the Caspian to the interior of Africa, numbering from *one hundred and twenty millions* to *one hundred and fifty millions* of immortal beings.

Taking these circumstances into account, the Committee agree that while it is *important*, it is *desirable* that the work solicited by the Mission should be accomplished.

While viewing the matter thus, the Committee are met by the fact that the present financial condition of the Society does not seem to warrant the assumption of the responsibility involved in undertaking the entire work at once, but warns us to proceed cautiously by arrangements for electrotyping such portions or forms as may be most urgently called for, to such extent as the means of the Society will allow, trusting and believing that the friends of the Society, so soon as the subject can be brought before them, will supply the means for completing the whole, as recommended by the Syrian Mission.

The Committee accordingly recommend the adoption of the following resolutions:

1. *Resolved*, That the completion of the version of the sacred Scriptures in the Arabic tongue by the American Missionaries in Syria, and widely approved by the best scholars in the East, is a subject for universal thanksgiving among the friends of Bible circulation.

2. *Resolved*, That the electrotyping of this version in the forms recommended by the Syrian Mission is a work in the highest degree important and desirable, and may well be undertaken by the American Bible Society.

3. *Resolved*, That while the present condition of our Treasury does not encourage the assumption of the responsibility involved in attempting at once the whole series desired by the Mission, the Secretaries, General Agent, and Publication Committee be, and are hereby authorized to make the necessary arrangements for electrotyping four sets of plates which the Committee on Versions may regard as most proper to be first undertaken.

4. *Resolved*, That the Secretaries of this Society be, and are hereby authorized to ask of the American Board of Commissioners of Foreign Missions the release of Dr. Van Dyck from their service for the time necessary to superintend the work.

5. *Resolved*, That if such release be granted, Rev. Dr. Van Dyck be invited to come to this country, at the expense of the American Bible Society, bringing with him his son to act as his assistant in superintending the electrotyping in the Bible House.

6. *Resolved*, That as for the completion of this great work, as recommended by the Syrian Mission, this Society must rely on the liberality of the friends of Bible circulation, the Secretaries be, and are hereby requested to present it in all its importance to the Christian Churches and our Auxiliaries as far as practicable throughout our country, in such modes as may, with the Divine blessing, secure all needed funds.

I. EXTRACTS FROM THE REPORT OF THE COMMITTEE ON MAKING DUPLICATE PLATES OF THE ARABIC BIBLE FOR THE BRITISH AND FOREIGN BIBLE SOCIETY.

"Let us furnish to our British friends all the plates they require, and let us accord to them the largest liberty to print and to circulate wherever there are human hands to receive them, or souls to be saved by their blessed truths. This will, we think, be the performance of only a sacred duty—the discharge merely of a sacred trust. But will it not be something besides? will it not be another recognition of that sacred brotherhood in our glorious Bible work, of which our British brethren were so generously and so promptly mindful in those dark days as we were entering upon the struggle for our nation's life?"

* * * * *

"These are the views which the Committee think have a bearing upon the particular question referred to them by the Board; but they likewise feel that there is one broad and comprehensive fact which underlies and controls this entire subject. It is this:

"That God in his providence has committed the guardianship and circulation of his Blessed Word to the two great Protestant nations of the earth and to the two national Societies as the instruments of carrying out this purpose. Our field is the world. 'The seed is the Word of God.' No particular part of this broad work belongs of right to either Society exclusively, except so far as God in his providence may afford to one a more ready access and greater facilities than to the other. But in this great work of evangelizing the world we should press forward side by side, with one heart and one purpose. Neither should they 'call aught of the things they possess their own;' but all things should be in 'common,' and all for the Master's use. Translations should be used interchangeably, and any advantage or facility secured by one Society should be a gain to the Cause and to all who love it. In this way alone can we accomplish most for the salvation of a dying world, and in this way best secure the blessing of Him whose truths we both desire to spread, and whom we both desire to serve."

The following are the resolutions of the Board of Managers on this subject:

Resolved, That we most cordially accede to the request of the British and Foreign Bible Society, and will make for them duplicate electrotype plates of such editions of the Arabic Scriptures now in course of preparation by us as they may designate, without charge.

Resolved, That our compliance with this request of the British and Foreign Bible Society be accompanied by the largest liberty for the free and unrestricted use of these plates, with their own imprint, conditioned only, that no alteration be made in the plates without the consent of this Society.

II. RESPONSE OF THE COMMITTEE OF THE BRITISH AND FOREIGN BIBLE SOCIETY, DATED LONDON, APRIL 16, 1866.

Resolved, That the committee have received with peculiar satisfaction the noble offer of the American Bible Society to present to this society, free of charge, duplicate electrotype plates of such editions of the Arabic translation of the Scriptures prepared by the Rev. Dr. Van Dyck, as the committee may select from the series which it is intended to issue in connexion with the Jubilee of the American Bible Society; and the committee, while accepting the liberal proposal, desire heartily to reciprocate the kind and Christian sentiments by which it has been dictated, and to convey to the Board of the American Bible Society the assurance of their warmest gratitude for the generosity evinced in regard to the work in question, and trust that the transaction, so honourable to those with whom it originates, may tend to strengthen the many friendly ties which unite the two Societies in their great enterprise of Scripture circulation throughout the world.

A SPECIMEN OF THE TYPE USED FOR THE NEW ARABIC BIBLE, translated by the REV. DOCTORS ELI SMITH and C. V. A. VAN DYCK, of the Syria Mission, A.B.C.F.M. Begun by DR. SMITH in 1847, and finished by DR. VAN DYCK, August, 1864. Punches, matrices, types, and electrotype plates, made by the American Bible Society, at the Bible House, Astor Place, New York. This work commenced August, 1865. First plate electrotyped March 15, 1866. Gen. xxxi. 22-33.

التكوين

الاصحاح الحادي والثلثون من ع ٢٢ الى ع ٣٣

٢٢ فأُخبِرَ لابان في اليوم الثالث بان يعقوب قد هرب ٠ ٢٣ فاخذ
اخوتهُ معهُ وسعى وراءهُ مسيرة سبعة ايامٍ . فادركهُ في جبل جلعاد ٠
٢٤ واتى الله الى لابان الاراميّ في حلم الليل . وقال لهُ احترز من ان تكلّمَ
يعقوب بخيرٍ او شرٍّ ٠ ٢٥ فلحق لابان يعقوب ويعقوب قد ضرب خيمتهُ في
الجبل . فضرَب لابانُ مع اخوتهِ في جبل جلعاد
٢٦ وقال لابان ليعقوب ماذا فعلتَ وقد خدعتَ قلبي وسقت
بناتي كسبايا السيف ٠ ٢٧ لماذا هربت خفيةً وخدعتني ولم تخبرني حتى
اشيّعك بالفرح والاغاني بالدفّ والعود ٠ ٢٨ ولم تدَعْني اقبّل بنيَّ وبناتي .
الآن بغباوةٍ فعلت ٠ ٢٩ في قدرة يدي ان اصنع بكم شرًّا . ولكن اله ابيكم
كلّمني البارحة قائِلاً احترز من ان تكلّم يعقوب بخيرٍ او شرٍّ ٠ ٣٠ والآن
انت ذهبت لانك قد اشتقت الى بيت ابيك . ولكن لماذا سرقت آلهتي
٣١ فاجاب يعقوب وقال للابان اني خفت لاني قلت لعلك
تغتصب ابنتيك مني ٠ ٣٢ الذي تجد آلهتك معهُ لا يعيش . قدام اخوتنا
انظر ماذا معي وخذهُ لنفسك ٠ ولم يكن يعقوب يعلم ان راحيل سرقتها
٣٣ فدخل لابان خباء يعقوب وخباء ليئة وخباء الجاريتين ولم يجد .

(D) THE BIBLE HOUSE.

"In 1851 the inability of the Managers to enlarge their operations so as to meet the increasing demands for the Scriptures induced them to appoint a special committee for the purpose of procuring suitable grounds for a new and larger edifice. This Committee consisted of Pelatiah Perit, Norman White, Charles N. Talbot, George D. Phelps, and A. Robertson Walsh, Esqs. As a number of contiguous lots were required, and in an accessible locality with an abundance of light and air, the Committee for a time were baffled in their efforts, and not a little disheartened. At length their attention was called to a plot of ground near the now central part of the City, which seemed to be peculiarly adapted to the object they sought. The same impression was made on the minds of the Board generally, and indeed, on all friends who gave the matter an examination. As another has observed: 'Thrice had this site been appropriated to other and far different uses, and thrice had the arrangements signally failed on consummation. An overruling Providence seems to have reserved it for its own present and higher purposes.'

"The entire plot was purchased, consisting of nearly twelve lots, or three quarters of an acre, and the Building Committee appointed to arrange without delay, for covering the whole with a substantial house. This Committee consisted of George D. Phelps, Norman White, Charles N. Talbot, A. Robertson Walsh, and James Suydam, Esqs., Managers, with the Hon. Luther Bradish, one of the Vice Presidents.

"On the 29th June, 1852, the corner stone of the new building was laid in the presence of a large assembly. Prayer was offered by the Rev. Nathan Bangs, D.D.; portions of the 119th Psalm were read by Rev. Dr. Ferris, and addresses delivered by the President, the Hon. Theodore Frelinghuysen, Rev. Dr. Spring, Hon. Luther Bradish, and the Rev. Dr. Stiles. The following books and documents were deposited in the corner stone: 1st, copy of one of the first Bibles published by the Society in 1817; 2d, copy of the last Bible published in 1852; 3d, the thirty-six Annual Reports of the Society, in four volumes; 4th, the Bible Society Record of the last three years; 5th, catalogue of the Society's Library; 6th, Report of the Committee on Versions in relation to the late collation of the English Bible; 7th, Report of the Board in regard to the principles of making translations; 8th, a programme of the exercises of this occasion, with a copy of the President's Address."

DESCRIPTION OF THE BUILDING.

"The Building Committee thus describe: It is bounded by the Fourth Avenue, Astor Place, Third Avenue, and Ninth Street, and is six stories high, with cellars and vaults.

"The front on Fourth Avenue is one hundred and ninety-eight feet nine inches; on Astor Place, two hundred and two feet, ten inches; on the Third

Avenue, seventy-six feet, eleven inches, and on Ninth Street, two hundred and thirty-two feet, six inches, and fifty feet in depth, having a large area in the centre. The cellars are eight feet six inches high; the first story, twelve feet; the second story, thirteen feet; the third story, eleven feet; the fourth story, ten feet four inches; the fifth story, ten feet; the sixth story, nine feet four inches; all in the clear between floors and ceilings.

"The fronts on Fourth Avenue and Astor Place are divided into five sections each. The two ends and centre sections have a projection of twelve inches in front, and also extend above the intermediate sections; and there is also a centre section to the front on Ninth Street, with a projection of twelve inches. The principal entrance on Fourth Avenue is decorated with four round columns with Corinthian capitals and moulded vases resting upon panels, and moulded pedestals and semi-circular arches are placed between the columns to form the heads of doors, etc., and all surmounted with a heavy cornice and segment pediment. The whole of the building is faced with Philadelphia pressed brick, and surmounted by a cornice formed with ornamental trusses, blocks, panels, etc. The centre section on Fourth Avenue and also the centre section on Ninth Street and Astor Place have segment pedestals. There are four principal entrances to the building, besides others for the operatives. A portion of the first, second, and third stories is arranged to be let for offices and stores until the Society may need them. The Managers' Room is located on the second story on Fourth Avenue, and is thirty feet wide by fifty feet deep, perfectly fire-proof, and lighted by a dome. The room is twenty-five feet high. Immediately underneath is the room for bound volumes of letters and library, also perfectly fire-proof.*

"The boilers are placed in the inner area or yard, so as not to expose the operatives to danger in case of accident. The press room occupies the fifth and sixth stories on Ninth Street, and is one hundred and nineteen feet long by forty-one feet in width. The whole establishment is so planned that, from the delivery of the paper in Ninth Street, it proceeds regularly through its various stages of manufacture until it arrives in books in the Depository, with but very little labour in hoisting from one story to another. Great attention has been paid to the subject of heating and ventilating the various departments.† In this respect, as well as in all others, the Committee have aimed to erect a building adapted in all its parts to the purposes for which it is wanted, and worthy of the Holy Book for whose universal dissemination the American Bible Society is labouring.

"This noble edifice, erected for the best of all purposes and at a considerable expense (some $300,000 with the ground), has not, as the Managers

* Underneath this room are two strongly built arched vaults, one of which is used as a workshop by the engineer, the other as a depository for stereotype and electrotype plates.

† To accomplish the former purpose, there are throughout the building more than ten miles of steam pipe.

would emphatically state, been put up at the cost of those in city or country who gave their funds for Bible distribution."—*Dr. Strickland's History.*

(E) EXECUTIVE OFFICERS.

The Society, since its organization, has had seven *presidents*, to wit: in 1816, Hon. Elias Boudinot; in 1821, Hon. John Jay; in 1828, Hon. Richard Varick; in 1831, Hon. John Cotton Smith; in 1846, Hon. Theodore Frelinghuysen; in 1862, Hon. Luther Bradish; and in 1864, James Lenox, Esq.

It has had seventy-five *vice presidents* in different periods of its history, comprising some of the most distinguished laymen of the country.

The following have acted as its *secretaries*, to wit: Rev. J. M. Mason, D.D.; Rev. J. B. Romeyn, D.D.; John Pintard, LL.D.; Rev. James Milnor, D.D.; Rev. S. S. Woodhull, D.D.; Rev. Thomas M'Auley, D.D., LL.D.; Rev. Charles G. Somers; Rev. Nathan Bangs, D.D.; Rev. John C. Brigham, D.D.; Robert F. Winslow, Esq.; Rev. Spencer H. Cone, D.D.; Rev. Edmund S. Janes, D.D.; Rev. Noah Levings, D.D.; Rev. S. Ireneus Prime, D.D.; Rev. Joseph Holdich, D.D.; Rev. Joseph C. Stiles, D.D.; Rev. James H. M'Neill; Rev. Wm. J. R. Taylor, D.D.; and Rev. T. Ralston Smith.

The *treasurers* of the Society, in their order, are as follows: in 1816, Hon. Richard Varick; in 1820, Wm. W. Woolsey, Esq.; in 1828, John Adams, Esq.; in 1832, Garret N. Bleeker, Esq., for five months; in 1832, Hubert Van Wagenen, Esq.; in 1836, John Nitchie, Esq.; in 1838, Abraham Keyser, Esq.; and in 1840, William Whitlock, Jr., Esq.

In the year 1839, Joseph Hyde, Esq., was appointed the Society's *General Agent* and *Assistant Treasurer*.

In the year 1853, Mr. Henry Fisher was appointed *Assistant Treasurer;* and in 1854, Mr. Caleb T. Rowe was appointed *General Agent*.

Of these officers a marked proportion have passed to their eternal rest. To those clerical Brethren known to me and with whom I have had relations more or less particular, it is decorous that I pay my tribute of respect and affection in this connexion.

The Rev. John M. Mason, S. T. P., stands out with special prominence as one of the strongest men our country has produced. Blest with unusual powers of mind, and enjoying every facility for their cultivation in this country and abroad, as he entered on his ministerial work he called out universal admiration as the successor of a venerated father in the pastoral office. As a pulpit orator he has had no superior; as a Professor of Theology he possessed such a faculty of condensing thought, and a clearness and precision of statement, and power of argument with a wide range of view, that his instructions were esteemed invaluable. As a college instructor in the higher classics, both Latin and Greek, he was unrivalled; for to thorough scholarship and the nicest appreciation of the characteristics of each author read by his classes, he added a remarkable power of illustration. He was of a warm, generous, confiding nature, ready always to sympathize with sorrow, although his noble form and the dignified movement which his Maker had given him led some to think he was cold and haughty. He was truly a laborious man (his friends thought unwisely so); at the time the Bible Society was formed he was the pastor of a large church and congregation, and conducted his two Sabbatical services; he was a Theological professor, and was punctually in his place; and in the office of Provost of Columbia College he had charge of the senior class in Latin and Greek, and was rarely a moment out of time: and these were his services for years, while besides he had all the usual duties of a pastor out of the pulpit, with many engagements and calls incidental to his high position. It pleased God to spare him for years to see the increasing prosperity of our Society, whose powerful and matchless appeal to the Christians of our country came from his pen. At length his system gave way under the pressure on it, his mind was impaired, though he to the last was able to bear his testimony to the truth, and died in the bosom of his family.

Rev. John B. Romeyn, D.D., the first Recording Secretary, was the beloved pastor of the Cedar Street Church, the parent flock of the Church on University Place and 10th Street, and that of the Church on 19th Street and 5th Avenue. In 1816 he was in his prime, being one of the most animated and captivating preachers in the city, around whom numerous young men of New England origin gathered, and known in his Presbyterial relations as a man of great executive ability and business tact, and promptness. He was regarded as one of the most influential clergymen in the Presbyterian Church in our country. His family was of Holland origin, and himself one of a succession of ministers in a family, which at the present time in its branches has a strong representation in the pulpit of the fourth or fifth generation. He is especially remembered as the author of a Report to the General Assembly of his church, which is to-day quoted as authority on the duty of the Church to her children. He was a man of great activity of mind, as well as of personal habits, and was a most important man to the Bible Society.

Rev. Dr. Thomas M'Auley, D.D., LL.D., came to the pastoral office in this city from the Professorship of Mathematics in Union College, enjoying a high reputation for varied scholarship and success as an instructor, and great eloquence as a preacher. Soon his power was felt, and he was honoured not only with a densely crowded audience, but with large increase to the communion of his church. He was indefatigable in all the details of pastoral work, and especially in the successful maintenance of a large Bible class for adults. The Bible Society had no warmer or more untiring friend, or one more ready for any emergency than he. For years he stood in the foreground of active workers, and as a representative of our Society was warmly greeted wherever he went to plead our Cause. In his latter years he was a subject of great infirmity.

The Rev. Selah S. Woodhull, D.D., was connected with the Reformed Protestant Dutch Church, and a pastor in Brooklyn, L. I., at the time of his appointment as Secretary He ranked with the foremost in his denomination, and for some time occupied a place in the service of the General Synod, which first called out his admirable administrative abilities, and proved him a capital business man. As a preacher he was clear, precise, and pointed, and won for himself the confidence of some of the best men in Brooklyn, who personally or through their families to a degree became in time the nucleus of the great church expansion which has occurred in Brooklyn. He brought his methodical excellence into his Secretaryship, and carried the work to a still higher degree of success. His reports were clear, suggestive, and always attentively heard. The General Synod of his church, estimating highly his ability, appointed him its Professor of Pastoral Theology in the Seminary at New Brunswick, N. J. He entered on his new work with great earnestness, and was beginning to realize a proportionate success, when the Master took him to himself.

The REV. NATHAN BANGS, D.D., was one of the leading spirits of the Methodist Episcopal Church, in which he filled some of the most responsible positions. For several years he was one of the chief Managers of the Publishing House in Mulberry Street, and successively editor of the Christian Advocate and Journal, the chief official organ of his church, and of the Methodist Quarterly Review; for several years Corresponding Secretary of the Missionary Society, and finally, President of the Wesleyan University. He was one whom his own denomination delighted to honour for his fidelity to its interests and the good service he rendered, while at the same time he delighted to behold and to acknowledge Christian character and action in other churches, and to contribute his portion in doing good in any department of Christian effort. Few men have commanded a wider influence or have been more extensively known. His Christian character grew in interest, and matured more and more with advancing age, until he was gathered into the heavenly garner like a shock of corn fully ripe. From his long residence in this City and his marked appearance, he was very generally recognized, and few men have been more missed in our community. He died on the 12th day of April, 1862, aged eighty-four years.

In the month of June, 1844, the Rev. E. S. JANES having been elected Bishop in the Methodist Church, the Rev. NOAH LEVINGS, D.D., was elected in his place Financial Secretary. He was very highly esteemed, not only in his own denomination, but by the Christian public generally. He possessed a warm Christian heart, a fertile mind, a vivid imagination, and a natural eloquence that rendered him always welcome and generally effective in advocating the Cause of the Society. He travelled very extensively in all parts of the country on his official business, making more than one extended journey to the West and South. In the Autumn of 1848, he made his last tour, travelling nearly four thousand miles over very bad roads and through much exposure to the weather and other inconveniencies. Under the pressure his health gave way, but he still persevered in his mission until the 24th of December, when he preached his last sermon in the Presbyterian Church at Natchez. From this he endeavoured to reach home, but he was able to get no further than Cincinnati. Here, at the house of a kind friend, he breathed his last on the 9th day of January, 1849.

It is not undeserving of notice in this place, that when some one in the course of his illness placed a large Bible under his pillow to raise his head, observing the letters on the back, he exclaimed: "Thou blessed book; lamp to my feet and light to my path; thou guide of my youth, director of my manhood, and support of my declining years; how cheerless would this world be were it not for thy Divine revelations and Christian promises." Thus died Noah Levings, in full faith of the Redeemer whom he loved and served, and to the circulation of whose Sacred Word he had devoted his last years. The truths he had promulgated with ability and success, sustained and cheered him in his final hours.

The Rev. John C. Brigham, D.D., was the first Corresponding Secretary whose entire time was given to the office, all his predecessors having sustained pastoral responsibilities, and necessarily dividing their time between the two offices.

The change was indispensable both as regarded the men themselves, pressed with heavy pastoral duty, and the rapidly expanding work of the Society, which has indeed so increased, that three Secretaries find their hands full, and the calls of duty multiplying.

Dr. Brigham came into the office with all the qualifications which a careful and extended education could give him, to which was added a large acquaintance with the wants of our field, both in the United States and the South American Peninsula, and a very extended acquaintance with the clergy. Few men will be found in any department of life of greater, far-seeing wisdom and more thoroughly balanced mind than he possessed. He was especially skilled in the knowledge of men, and would succeed where difficulties and entanglements and opposition would discourage ordinary men.

Long was he spared to us, though being tried in his last year by infirm health, his work was limited mostly to consultations and advice. His loss was deeply felt, though his influence and faithful work will continue to bless men.

Rev. James Milnor, D.D., was invited in the summer of 1816, to become the rector of St. George's Church in this City, and in September entered upon his parochial duty, and soon connected himself with the various benevolent societies which began their work about that time. His parish and he were animated with the same spirit of liberal action, and stood with the foremost in the Sunday school work, then enlisting the interest and energies of the churches in the City. He became the second President of the New York Sunday School Union, and for a number of years occupied that place to the satisfaction of all. As a preacher, he was distinguished for the highly intellectual as well as truly evangelical character of his services, and was heard with great gratification by multitudes beside his immediate parishioners. From the organization of the American Tract Society, in which he took a leading part, he occupied for a long period the chairmanship of its executive committee, and down to his death that of its most important committee on Publication, where soundness of judgment was especially required. With warm preference for his own form of church order, he was of most catholic spirit, and always maintained intimate Christian fellowship with clergymen of other churches. He became connected with the American Bible Society, directly after removed to this City, and after serving for one year as Secretary for Domestic Correspondence, succeeded Dr. Mason as Foreign Corresponding Secretary, and occupied that responsible place in connexion with his pastoral duties for twenty years. For many years he was chairman of the Committee on Versions. His removal by death created a deep sensation throughout all the churches, for all felt that he belonged to the cause of piety.

The Rev. Spencer H. Cone, D.D., of the Baptist Church, must be pronounced a rare man, whether his breaking away from the fascinations of a highly successful stage career for the Gospel of Jesus Christ, or his careful and thorough self-tuition in theology, or his eloquence in the pulpit and on all public occasions be considered. It is not too emphatic to say he stood with the strongest men of his denomination at the time of his official relation with us, and in his work as a minister was blest with seeing church after church built up through his instrumentality. He felt it his duty to separate from our ranks in consequence of the action on the versions made by several of his missionary Brethren in the East, which all his fellow labourers with whom he had often taken sweet counsel regretted, but in their obligation to the catholic principles of our Constitution could not remedy. His personal friend and brother in the Baptist faith, President Wayland, of Brown University, joined in that regret, while he expressed fully his agreement with the course of action adopted.

Dr. Wayland's account closes thus:

Dr. Milnor's preamble and resolutions, with the addition suggested by Dr. Sharp, were passed by the Board, and to the best of my knowledge, form at present the rule of its proceedings in respect to versions of the Scriptures in foreign languages. They are in these words:

"By the Constitution of the American Bible Society, its Managers are, in the circulation of the Holy Scriptures, restricted to such copies as are without note or comment, and, in the English language, to the version in common use. The design of this restriction seems to have been to simplify and mark out the duties of the Society, so that all the religious denominations of which it is composed might harmoniously unite in the performance of these duties.

"As the Managers are now called to aid extensively in circulating the Sacred Scriptures in languages other than the English, they deem it their duty in conformity with the obvious spirit of their compact, to adopt the following resolutions as the rule of their conduct in making appropriations for the circulation of the Scriptures in foreign tongues:

"1. *Resolved*, That in appropriating money for the translation, printing, and distribution of the Sacred Scriptures in foreign languages, the Managers feel at liberty to encourage only such versions as conform, in the principles of their translation, to the common English version, at least so far that all the religious denominations represented in this Society can consistently use and circulate said versions in their several schools and communities.

"2. *Resolved*, That a copy of the above Preamble and Resolution be sent to each of the Missionary Boards accustomed to receive pecuniary grants from this Society, with the request that the same may be transmitted to their several missionary stations where the Scriptures are in the process of translation; and also that the said several Missionary Boards be informed that their application for aid be accompanied with a declaration that the versions which they propose to circulate are executed in accordance with the above resolution."

I close with the declaration that I cannot perceive how, consistently with the principles of its Constitution, the Bible Society could have adopted any other rule. It is equally required by the dictates of justice and of common sense, and it breathes the spirit of fraternal equality and Christian courtesy. It has therefore my cheerful and unwavering support.

F. Wayland.

With all this, we give Dr. Cone the meed of high praise in his able and eminently useful ministerial work.

(F) RESUPPLY.

The resolutions of the Board marking out the labour to be entered on in the new half century, which Dr. Spring seconded, and in behalf of which he made his most touching speech, which has been referred to, were as follows:

Whereas, God in his gracious providence has conducted this Society from small beginnings to a degree of strength and capability which fit it for accomplishing a greater work than ever, and has signalized our Jubilee year as a year of peace and universal freedom throughout our land: and

Whereas, it appears, from the correspondence of our Secretaries, that multitudes throughout our older States are found destitute of the Word of Life: and

Whereas, through the desolations of war, great want of the Scriptures exists in the South and Southwest, and the means of supplying it by former Bible organizations there existing have been swept away: and

Whereas, millions of freedmen, now thrown upon their own efforts and passing through a most critical formative state, need the great charter of duty and privileges, and are anxiously asking for it:

Resolved, That while this Society feels deeply its obligations to the world, and will go on in its work abroad, it is clearly the duty of the American Bible

Society and its numerous friends to respond to these indications of what God would have us to do, by at once entering upon the supply of this vast field of want.

Resolved, That it is highly befitting that this should be the first work of our second semi-century.

Resolved, That with the aid of the gracious Head, which has done so much for us in the past, we will without delay undertake this truly American work, and call upon all lovers of the Bible and our country to unite with us.

At the late Jubilee Anniversary of this Institution, which was held in the Academy of Music, May 10th, 1866, the following resolution was unanimously adopted by the Society:

Resolved, That, relying upon the providence and grace of the Almighty God, this Society hereby approves the resolutions adopted by the Board of Managers at their last meeting, to undertake without delay a third general supply of the whole country with the Word of God—a work which is eminently befitting us as an acknowledgment of Divine goodness in the past, and a proper beginning of our second half century.

At the regular meeting of the Board of Managers, held July 2d, 1866, they adopted unanimously the subjoined *plan for accomplishing this great work:*

1. *Resolved*, That it be earnestly recommended to the local Bible societies throughout the country to adopt measures for supplying with the Bible, as early as practicable, all destitute families within their respective limits.

2. *Resolved*, That, in prosecuting this work, regard should also be had to children and youth, who have great need of the Scriptures for Sabbath school and other purposes, and who should be furnished with the New Testament, at least, as far as possible.

3. *Resolved*, furthermore, That seamen, boatmen, railroad hands, stage drivers, etc., who are favoured with few Sabbath privileges, have increased necessity for the written Word of God, and should be furnished with it; and that special attention should be given to the supply of the freed people of the South, in their schools, families, churches, etc.

4. *Resolved*, That in entering on the proposed undertaking, it will be for the benefit of all concerned, that a portion at least of the funds required for the purchase of books be raised and forwarded when orders for books are made. The Parent Society will thus be furnished with ready means for preparing books with economy, and the auxiliaries saved from a protracted, disheartening debt.

5. *Resolved*, That in effecting the proposed supply by the auxiliaries, it is desirable that the work be performed, as far as possible, by self-denying volunteers, each taking an assigned district; and that when hired labourers are necessary, they be sustained, as far as practicable, by the local societies; and aid from the Parent Society, when needed, be sought in the way of books, rather than funds, for colportage.

6. *Resolved*, That the various auxiliaries, as they enter on the proposed supply, be requested to inform this Board when they commence their labours, and also furnish the results when the work is completed, that the same may be published in the Bible Society Record and Annual Reports.

7. *Resolved*, That in portions of the country where auxiliaries cannot be found, or relied on for supplying the destitute, the Committees on Distribution and on Agencies be instructed to adopt such other methods for securing a supply as may be deemed most expedient and effective.

(G) ANNIVERSARY ADDRESSES.

JUBILEE YEAR.

THE American Bible Society held its Fiftieth Annual Meeting at the Bible House, in Astor Place, on Thursday, May 10, 1866, at nine o'clock, A. M.

James Lenox, Esq., President, in the chair, assisted by the following Vice Presidents: Hon. Peter D. Vroom, of New Jersey; John Tappan, Esq., of Massachusetts; Hon. A. B. Hasbrouck and William Whitlock, Jr., Esq., of New York; Hon. Robert C. Winthrop, of Massachusetts; Norman White and Frederick S. Winston, Esqs., of New York; Gen. William Williams, of Connecticut; and James Suydam, Esq., of New York.

The Rev. J. T. Peck, D.D., of California, read the 111th Psalm, and offered prayer.

Caleb T. Rowe, Esq., General Agent, read the Minutes of the previous meeting of the Society, and they were approved.

He then reported the names of nine Managers, composing the fourth class, whose term of office expired at that time, viz.:

Frederick T. Peet,	Edward J. Woolsey,
Isaac Wood, M. D.,	Robert Carter,
Cornelius Du Bois,	Marshall S. Bidwell,
Washington R. Vermilye,	Chandler Starr,

Richard P. Buck.

A Committee, composed as follows, was appointed by the Chair to nominate suitable persons to fill vacancies: Charles Tracy, Esq., Rev. Dr. Rodgers, of N. J., Rev. Dr. Butler, of Mass., Schureman Halsted, Esq., and Theophilus A. Brouwer, Esq.

The Committee, after due consideration, reported for re-election those whose term of office had just expired.

The report was adopted, and the gentlemen named were declared duly elected Managers for four years, ending May, 1870.

On motion of the Rev. Dr. Canfield, of Brooklyn, it was

Resolved, That the new Board of Managers be directed to meet at the Bible House, in New York, on the third Thursday in this present month, for the purpose of organizing for the ensuing year.

On motion of Chandler Starr, Esq., of Conn., it was

Resolved, That when the Society adjourn, it do adjourn to meet at the Bible House, in New York, on the second Thursday in May, 1867, at nine o'clock, A. M.

The following delegates from foreign countries, and from our auxiliary societies, were reported as present:

Rev. Thomas Phillips and Rev. Thomas Nolan, from the British and Foreign Bible Society; Rev. Cesar Pascal, from the Bible Society of France; Rev. Lachlin Taylor, D.D., and Rev. William Ormiston, D.D., from the Bible Society of Upper Canada; Rev. Benjamin P. Stone, D.D., from the New Hampshire Bible Society; Rev. Daniel Butler and the Hon. Robert C. Winthrop, from the Massachusetts Bible Society; Rev. Dennis Platt, from the South Norwalk Bible Society, Conn.; Theophilus A. Brouwer, Esq., President New York City Bible Society; Archibald M'Clure, Esq., President, Rev. David Dyer, and Rev. Alfred A. Farr, from Albany County Bible Society, N. Y.; James Rider, Esq., and Rev. J. M. Van Buren, Long Island Bible Society; Rev. A. B. Lambert, President, and Dr. James Savage, from Washington County Bible Society, N. Y.; John Lyon, Esq., President, and Rev. E. W. Bentley, Secretary, from Ulster County Bible Society, N. Y.; Rev. L. H. Van Dyck, from Montgomery County Bible Society, N. Y.; Rev. Robert Everett, from Remsen and Steuben Welsh Bible Society, N. Y.; Ira H. Cobb and Timothy Hough, Esqs., from Onondaga County Bible Society, N. Y.; Rev. Dr. Paddock, from Broome County Bible Society, N. Y.; Rev. Thomas Jenkins, from Utica Welsh Bible Society, N. Y.; Hon. R. H. Cuyler and Hon. Charles Hathaway, from Delaware County Bible Society, N. Y.; Rev. Wilson Phraner and Rev. S. I. Prime, D.D., from Westchester County Bible Society, N. Y.; Rev. R. K. Rodgers, D.D., from Somerset County Bible Society, N. J.; Hon. B. F. Randolph, President, and Rev. B. C. Taylor, D.D., from Hudson County Bible Society, N. J.; Rev. D. L. King and Rev. R. T. Middleditch, from Monmouth County Bible Society, N. J.; D. C. English, Esq., from Middlesex County Bible Society, N. J.; Rev. S. M. Hammill, D.D., from Laurenceville Bible Society, N. J.; Rev. J. V. R. Hughes and Wm. French, Esq., from Nassau Hall Bible Society, N. J.; Rev. S. W. Hilyard and R. T. Haines, Esq., from Union County Bible Society, N. J.; Rev. A. M. Palmer and William Rankin, Esq., from Essex County Bible Society, N. J.; Adam Stiger, Esq., from Hunterdon County Bible Society, N. J.; Rev. J. M. Ogden, from Morris County Bible Society, N. J.; Rev. I. H. Torrence and Willard Hall, Esq., from Pennsylvania Bible Society; Rev. D. H. Emerson, from Delaware State Bible Society; Rev. T. V. Moore, D.D., from Virginia Bible Society; Rev. J. T. Peck, D.D., President California Bible Society.

The Society then proceeded to the Academy of Music, corner of Fourteenth Street and Irving Place, to celebrate its Fiftieth Anniversary and Jubilee year. James Lenox, Esq., President of the Society, took the chair at ten o'clock.

The Rev. E. P. Rogers, D.D., of New York, read the 148th Psalm, and offered prayer.

The President delivered a brief and eloquent address.

The Rev. GARDINER SPRING, D.D., of New York, moved the adoption of the first resolution:

Resolved, That the Report, an abstract of which has been presented, be printed and circulated under the direction of the Board of Managers.

I should be ashamed of myself, Mr. President, and I am sure I should deserve the reproaches of this Christian assembly, notwithstanding the unexpected welcome with which they have greeted me as I rise to my feet, if I should occupy time which will be so much better employed by gentlemen whose voices are not so familiar to this auditory as mine.

Fifty years ago I stood as the youngest member of those who formed the American Bible Society. That has been a remarkable providence by which my own poor and unworthy life has been conducted up to the present hour; and I desire to give thanks to the God of heaven that I am permitted to pay this tribute at the footstool of his throne. Were I to utter any prolonged remarks, I would select for my text the words which Moses called the people of Israel to remember: "And thou shalt remember all the way which the Lord thy God led thee these forty years in the wilderness, to humble thee, and to prove thee, to know what was in thy heart," and "to do thee good at thy latter end."

But, sir, I am not to deserve your reproach for continuing these remarks. I have but a single thought; it is my earnest desire that the God of the Bible shall be honoured in your future career as He has been in some measure in the past.

May God be first, God last, and God every thing! All glory, as it was in the beginning, is now, and ever shall be, to the Father, Son, and Holy Ghost.

The Rt. Rev. CHARLES P. M'ILVAINE, D.D., of Ohio, made the following remarks:

I have one request to make of this assembly, since the affectionate and solemn words which our most venerated father has uttered, in all probability, have not been heard by the greater portion of the audience, in consequence of the feebleness of so advanced a period of life.

Our venerated father is one of only two survivors of the founders of the American Bible Society. He is the only one of the survivors capable of being present on this occasion. We are exceedingly happy that God has spared him to be present, and has given us the privilege of his presence, and to hear these devoted and solemn words from his lips. We know not what we shall be on the morrow at so advanced a period of life as our venerated father has attained.

It is hardly to be expected that when another anniversary of this Society shall occur, we shall have the privilege of thus meeting him, especially of hearing his words. We may therefore suppose that on this occasion, as on another, he has made his farewell address; and perhaps it is a little appropriate that I should say these few words, and make the request that I am going to make, because in all probability there are very few besides myself who, although not present at the formation of the American Bible Society, because too young to be in the ministry, were cognizant of all the events connected therewith. I saw the coming away from my native town in New Jersey of the Hon. John M. Wells, who presided over one of the first meetings, and the Hon. Judge Boudinot, one of my neighbours, who was the first President of the Society. Remembering those times, I may be permitted to mention the first occasion on which I ever saw or heard the voice of this our venerated friend. Just about that time, when I was a student in Princeton College and was attending the evening prayers (very likely Dr. Spring don't recollect it), at a time when there was a very great seriousness and religious impression in college, the president, the Rev. Dr. Greene, introduced to us one who seemed at that time in such feeble health that it could hardly have been expected he could have attained to so great an age.

He stood up before the students, and said these few words, which made a great impression on my mind, and always remained stereotyped on my memory. Said he: "Young gentlemen, I was present when I saw you to-day go to the refectory for your mid-day meal. I saw the greater number enter. By and by those who had lingered behind entered with difficulty; presently a few more straggling ones came, and the door was shut, and it was not opened to them, and they entered not in," and that shut door was the text of a short but exceedingly impressive discourse to us at that time. It has never passed, even the words of it, away from my remembrance.

Now, my dear friends, since we all are in these circumstances which I have just related, it does seem to many of us who have conversed one with another on this platform, that we should do something more to testify our respect for our valuable friend and father than simply to be silently the hearers of the words he has addressed to us, and spectators of his presence; and therefore, before the resolution is seconded or another word is heard, I request, and the request will be met with joy by all of us, that this audience rise in testimony of respect to Dr. Spring.

Immediately the vast audience rose, and remained standing for some time, in silence and in tears. The scene was most impressive.

The Rev. J. T. Peck, D.D., President of the California Bible Society, said:

Mr. President: In the name of one of the youngest, and I may venture to say one of the most vigorous of our auxiliaries, I rise by request to second the resolution offered by our venerated friend and father. I do it, sir, without remark.—The resolution was adopted.

The Rev. Rufus Anderson, D.D., of Massachusetts, moved the adoption of the second resolution. He said:

I have been requested to speak of the Bible in its connexion with the *unevangelical world*, having the following resolution to propose—

"That the Society acknowledges the goodness of God in the vast accession, during the past half century, to the means of Scriptural knowledge in the unevangelized portions of the world."

Mr. President: It is a grand peculiarity in Protestant missions, that in them *preaching* and the *Bible* go hand in hand. And since the Bible must be read in order to be useful, there is a third important element in our foreign missions, inseparably connected with Bible distribution, and that is *education.* The people must all be taught to read God's blessed Word. The Romish missions in China, Japan, and the African kingdom of Congo were conducted on a very extended scale, and for a time had proportionate results. But they withheld the Bible from the people; and their missions, not being founded on that *rock*, but on the *sand* of human tradition and authority, fell; and great was the fall thereof. And so it must be with every mission in which God's Word is not one of the primary agencies.

So deeply imbedded is this truth in the Protestant mind, that I sometimes have feared there may have been an undue proportion of our ablest missionaries employed heretofore in Scripture translations. But though Protestant missions may now have somewhat fewer converts, churches, and native preachers than if there had been more of preaching and familiar intercourse with the people, we have, nevertheless, this glorious result to rejoice over—worth more than a hundred millions of dollars—that the Inspired Oracles have been translated, transfused, during the past fifty years, into languages spoken over more than three fourths of the unevangelized world! To speak with more precision, the entire Bible, during this period, has been translated into *thirty-nine* languages, outside of Christendom, embracing nearly all the more extensive and important; the New Testament into *thirty-five* other tongues; and portions of Scripture into still *forty-eight* others: making *one hundred and twenty-two languages*, in the great field of Christian missions, that have been enriched and ennobled with portions at least of the Word of God, since the American Bible Society commenced its operations. And not a few of these languages had first to be reduced to a written form. These *translations* have been wrought out more especially by missionaries and missionary societies.

And we come now to the department of *printing* and *circulation*, which is almost exclusively the province of Bible societies. I find that the American Bible Society has placed more than $250,000 at the disposal of missionaries of the American Board alone, for printing and circulating the Scriptures, for which those missionaries and that Board are profoundly thankful. I have not the means of knowing how much it has placed at the disposal of missionaries of other societies; but I find that the sum total of your grants for foreign distribution, to a large extent in languages beyond the limits of the Christian world, falls but little if any short of $800,000. The appropriations by the British and Foreign Bible Society for giving the Scriptures to the unevangelized nations, during the past half century, I have estimated at $2,375,000; making a sum total for both societies of more than three millions. And it should be borne in mind that this is for countries beyond the bounds of Christendom, and since the origin of this Society.

How many *volumes* of Scripture, in whole or in part, have been printed in these languages and circulated during the time now under review is an inquiry to which I have not been able to find an answer entirely satisfactory. But this I know, that more than 1,600,000 copies were issued, in the languages of India alone, in the short space of ten years previous to 1862. I suppose that of the more than 80,000,000 of copies which have been issued by Bible societies since 1804, not less than 6,000,000 have been distributed among the nations lying outside of Christendom. And it is worthy of note, that this number is *double* the number of the Bibles believed to have existed in Christendom during the more than three centuries from the printing of the first Bible, in 1460, down to the era of Bible societies. And it is a far greater number than were in the hands of mankind, through all the centuries, from the time of Moses down to the Reformation; thus giving us a most impressive illustration of accelerated progress, in these modern times, in filling the unevangelized world with the means of Scriptural knowledge.

And what has been the *influence* upon the benighted nations of thus transfusing the Word of God into their spoken languages? It has been, sir, just what the lighting up of your "Central Park" is in a dark night. Night is not thereby converted into day. The distant looker-on sees no perceptible impression made upon the darkness. But the traveller in the Park finds his path illuminated, and goes on his way rejoicing. Precisely such is the influence of the Bible and of Christian missions in the benighted regions of heathenism—a light shining *in* the darkness, illuminating the pathway to heaven. There is no help like a good version of the Scriptures for a new missionary in acquiring a language. There is no argument so effective as the Scriptures for educating the masses. For every man, whatever his condition, has the same right to be taught to *read* the inspired Volume that he has to *own* it. The emancipated slaves, with the New Testament in their hands, may claim it as their chartered right from heaven to have schools for themselves and for their children. Every volume of Scripture is, indeed, an appeal from high Heaven in favour of universal education.

While experience has shown that the *Bible* and the *preacher* must ordinarily go together, in the enterprise for reclaiming the heathen world, now and then we light upon a fact which shows that the Holy Spirit sometimes operates on the pagan heart *by the printed volume alone*. Quite recently a well authenticated case of this kind has come to my knowledge. It was that of a young man at Yeddo, the capital of Japan, who seems never to have come in contact with a Christian missionary. This young Japanese somehow acquired a longing for foreign knowledge. His first book was an atlas of the United States, in the Chinese language, prepared by an American missionary, and he thus became greatly interested to know more of the institutions of our country.

One day, while examining the library of a friend, he found a small Chinese Bible, which he borrowed. He at once cordially received the Scripture account of creation, and of the coming of the Son of God into our world as the Saviour of men. He then resolved, if possible, to get possession of a Bible in the English language, and began the study of that language with a Japanese teacher, and his prayer to the God of the Bible was, that he might go where that language was spoken. Breaking away at length from the paternal home, on the plea that he belonged to the Heavenly Father and must believe Him, he got on board an American ship bound to Boston, and came to that port. His prayer on his arrival, as he has stated it, was in these words: "O God, if thou have got eyes, please look upon me! O God, if thou have got ears, please hear me! I long to read the Bible, and to be civilized by the Bible."

The prayer of this Bible convert—this trophy (as I doubt not) of your own Society—was heard and answered; for he received the generous patronage of the owner of the ship which brought him to our shores, and is now, I am happy to say, a student in one of our best New England academies; hoping one day to become a messenger of salvation, through the blood of the Lamb, to his benighted countrymen. And how natural to suppose that the same leaven may now be working in many a thoughtful mind, among the myriads in those crowded portions of the Eastern world!

But I must close. This Society is now electrotyping the Bible in the languages of the Sandwich Islanders and of the Arab race. How different those two peoples in point of numbers! the one having as many millions as the other has thousands. Yet I hardly know which of these two enterprises most interests my own mind. It is not long since thousands of the poor people of those far-off Western isles grasped this hand of mine, in my progress through the islands, in token of their Christian fellowship; and be assured, sir, that *they* will joyfully receive the beautiful volume of God's Word you are preparing to send them. As for the version in the Arabic language—now, or soon to be, in the process of electrotyping in as many as ten different forms—when the volumes shall all be laid upon your table, at a future meeting, in the reformed Arabic printed letter, emulating the most beautiful Arabic manuscript, they will justly be regarded as among the moral wonders and glories of the age.

Hon. Peter D. Vroom, of New Jersey, said:

I rise simply for the purpose of seconding the resolution which has been offered and so ably advocated. I second it with the prayer that the efforts which have been made for the circulation of the Scriptures will be successful.

Address of Hon. Robert C. Winthrop, of Massachusetts, before offering the third resolution.

I know too well, Mr. President, the value of time on such an occasion as this to allow myself to trepass long on your indulgence this morning. I could not find it in my conscience, however, to decline altogether the repeated requests of your Executive Committee that I would take some part in these Anniversary exercises. Indeed, I should have felt myself quite unworthy of being numbered among the Vice Presidents of this noblest of all Societies, had I willingly absented myself from your Jubilee to-day. Why, what a Jubilee it is, my friends, and how eminently worthy of observance by all who take an interest in the welfare of mankind! What other Jubilee—moral, social, literary, political, national—what other Jubilee is there to be compared with it, in view of the enduring influence and far-reaching extent of the work which it commemorates? What other association of men has a right to indulge in the same measure of joy and exultation which belongs to those who can look back on fifty years of faithful and successful labour, in publishing and circulating the Word of God?

I have often before, Mr. President, been deeply impressed with the doings of this Society, even in a single year, as I have found them described in some one of its Annual Reports, and as I have reflected on the influence which must have been produced by the thousands and tens of thousands of Bibles which have been distributed through its agency during a single revolution of the seasons. But as I contemplate to-day the aggregate results of the full half century which has elapsed since its original institution; as I look at the statements which have been made up fo u by your faithful Secretaries, and mark the grand sum tot of the facts and figures; as I think of more than twenty-one millions of volumes, containing a part or the whole of the Holy Scriptures, scattered broadcast over the world, wherever there was an eye to read them, a hand to receive them, or a heart to understand them, I confess I can conceive of nothing in the whole range of human effort or human accomplishment more worthy of being the subject of grateful acknowledgment to God, and of triumphant celebration among men. Oh, my friends! if we could ascertain at this moment something of the secret history of those twenty-one millions of volumes; if we could trace them back to the hands into which they first fell, and follow them down through all their successive uses and ownerships; if we could track them wherever they have gone, over sea and over land, many of them into the abodes of want and wretchedness, many of them into remote and barbarous lands, not a few of them into scenes of peril on the stormy deep, many of them into scenes of conflict and carnage on the battle fields of our own land, in that great struggle which, we thank God, has resulted in the rescue of our Union; if we could gather all the facts into a single focus, and perceive at a glance how many hearts they have gladdened and elevated, how many homes they have cheered and blessed, how many souls they have lighted and lifted on their way to the skies, how many noble lives they have inspired and animated, how many heroic deaths they have consoled and comforted—what a sublime record would be presented to us! What is there in all the regions of romance, or in the whole compass of the drama, that would equal it in interest? What is there in all the boasted achievements of real life that would approach it in importance?

Beyond all doubt, my friends, we are dealing here to-day with the great enginery of the world's progress, with the greatest of all instrumentalities for social advancement as well as for individual salvation. Personally or politically, whether as States and nations or as individual men and women, we can do without any thing and without every thing better than without the Bible. We could spare Homer from ancient literature; we could spare Shakspeare, and Milton too, from modern literature, and there would still be something, there would still be much left. But what an eclipse would be experienced, what an aching void would be felt, were there no Sermon on the Mount, no Gospel by St. John, no Psalms of David, no Prophecy of Isaiah, no Epistle to the Corinthians! Where would this world of ours have found itself by this time, had those Divine and matchless voices never been vouchsafed to us? Into what lower deeps, beyond the lowest depths which have ever yet been imagined, of superstition and sensuality, of vice, and villany, and barbarism, would it have been plunged! How should we have realized in such a case the full import of that agony which one of the old prophets intended to portray in those memorable words: "Behold, the days come that I will send a famine in the land, not a famine of bread, nor a thirst for water, but of hearing the words of the Lord: And they shall wander from sea to sea, and from the north even to the east, they shall run to and fro to seek the word of the Lord, and shall not find it!" God in his mercy spare our own land from such a famine as that! Better were it for us to endure war, or pestilence, or any other variety of famine, than a famine of the Word of the Lord.

Why, there are single books of the Bible—there are single chapters of the Bible—nay, there are single verses of the Bible, which are worth all that was ever written or uttered, before or since, by human pens or human lips. How well did the poet Cowper say, in one of his charming familiar letters—it was to Lady Hesketh, I believe—"'He that believeth on me is passed from death unto life,' though it be as plain a sentence as words can form, has more beauties in it than all the labours antiquity can boast of!" "Read me, read me," said Oliver Cromwell on his death-bed, "those verses from the fourth chapter of the Epistle to the Philippians, in which the apostle speaks of having learned, in whatsoever state he was, therewith to be content, for he could do all things through Christ who strengthened him. That Scripture," said the dying hero, "did once save my life, when my eldest son died, which went as a dagger to my heart; indeed it did." And each one of you, my friends, I doubt not, will readily recall other texts with which there are similar associations. Indeed, there is hardly any one to whom the Bible is at all familiar or at all precious, who has not some favourite chapter or verse which is the very life and joy of his soul.

But I may not detain you a moment longer with these general remarks. Let me only express the hope, that in some degree commensurate with the value we place on our own Bibles will be our willingness to contribute towards sending the Bible to others. I rejoice, Mr. President, that your Jubilee is not to pass off in mere empty words of congratulation and compliment, but that you have resolved to signalize it by at least two works of the highest interest and importance—one of them, the sending of the Bible to the freedmen of our own land, and the replenishing the supply of Bibles throughout the whole desolated and famishing South; the other, the publication, by a process than which there is nothing in the "Arabian Nights" more marvellous or more magical, of that Arabic version of the sacred Volume, by which it is to be brought home to one hundred and twenty millions of people, in those very regions of the earth in which its great scenes were originally transacted. And now, if there are men, or women, or children, within reach of my voice, who have not already contributed something—it may be of their abundance, or it may be of their penury, their two mites, if nothing more—towards these noble ends, I trust that this occasion will be the means of calling their attention to what ought to be regarded as alike the privilege and the duty of us all.

Let me hope, too, that when another Jubilee anniversary shall be celebrated, long after most of us shall have gone to our account, it may prove that the next half century will have been even more abundant in labours in this great Cause than that which has now closed, and that the whole Christian people of our land will see to it that those labours are not restrained or restricted by any deficiency of means in your treasury. I would not under-estimate the importance of other societies—the Tract Societies, and Sunday School Unions, and Domestic and Foreign Missionary Boards, which are engaged in kindred efforts to hasten the coming of the glorious day when the knowledge of the Lord shall cover the earth as the waters cover the seas. God bless and prosper them all! But even as the Bible stands alone, in measureless superiority, in peerless pre-eminence, above all other books, so have the societies which are devoted to its publication and distribution, pure and simple, without note or comment, a paramount claim upon the support, the sympathy, the cordial co-operation of all who profess and call themselves Christians.

It only remains for me to say, my friends, in fulfilment of the agreeable duty which has been assigned to me on this occasion, that we do not forget to-day, that during the whole existence of this Society, it has enjoyed the constant and friendly co-operation of that great British and Foreign Bible Society which was the immediate forerunner and exemplar of our own, and whose labours and accomplishments have been far greater than those we are assembled to commemorate. Whatever other bonds of sympathy between us and our old mother country may have been weakened or sundered—and we trust they will all be restored in their full strength at no distant day—let us rejoice that we still read and circulate the same Bible, in the same noble tongue, in the same majestic version. And most gladly do we hail the presence, on this occasion, of the delegates from that mother land and that mother society. There are delegates here, too, from the neighbouring British colonies. And I am glad to know that there is at least one delegate also from that sunny land from which came the precious Huguenot blood, which so many of us are proud to feel mingling at this moment with other currents in our own veins, and which quickened the pulses of the first two illustrious Presidents of this Society, Elias Boudinot and John Jay. I am sure you are all eager to manifest your gratification at the presence of these honoured and welcome guests, and that you will adopt by acclamation the resolution which it is now, in conclusion my privilege to offer:

Resolved, That we welcome to our Jubilee, with warm hearts and with cordial greetings, the representatives of sister institutions from England, France, Canada, and elsewhere; and that they be requested to communicate to their respective societies this assurance of our Christian fellowship and international efforts to send abroad the Bible "for the healing of the nations."

The delegates from the foreign Bible societies responded to the resolution in the following order:

Rev. THOMAS PHILLIPS, delegate from the British and Foreign Bible Society, spoke as follows:

Mr. President, Ladies and Gentlemen: Having the high honour of appearing among you this day as one of the representatives of the British and Foreign Bible Society, I must be allowed to say at the outset, and I do it without the least affectation, that while I greatly value the privilege, I am at the same time deeply sensible of the responsibility attached to the position in which, through the kindness of our committee, I have been placed.

Twelve years ago we celebrated the Jubilee of our society in England; and amongst the many delightful reminiscences of that year, we shall always think with pleasure of the visit paid us by your able delegates. The appointment of such men as the Rev. Dr. M'Ilvaine and Dr. Vermilye on that important mission conveyed to us the pleasing assurance, that on your side of the Atlantic a deep interest was felt in the world-wide operations of the great *Parent* Bible Society. My esteemed friend and myself are here to return that pleasant visit, and to convey to you, in the warmest and most expressive terms which we can find within the limits of language, the very sincere congratulations of our society on this interesting Jubilee occasion. We are here, sir, to unite with you most heartily in thanksgivings to Almighty God for the manifold blessings vouchsafed to the American Bible Society during the first fifty years of its existence and labours.

Without pretending to take the Jewish Jubilee as a model, it must be right and proper to take advantage of an opportunity like this, which may only occur once in a lifetime, for the purpose of carrying out practically certain high and holy and useful objects. I can testify from official knowledge and personal knowledge and personal observation, that our Jubilee year was one of the most hallowed and blessed seasons we have ever known. It seemed to be the right time to review the past, and to set out afresh and with redoubled zeal on a career of future usefulness. We can look back to the year of Jubilee as the commencement of a new era in our history, and the impulse given to the good Cause at that time is felt to this day.

We invited our Christian friends throughout the world to unite with us in commemorating the Divine goodness so abundantly vouchsafed to the society in its remarkable origin, early history, and rapid progress. We asked them to thank God with us for raising up such an institution when it was so much needed, for preserving it when it was so fiercely assailed, and for the marvellous success which accompanied its efforts in various departments of labour both at home and abroad—success beyond, very far beyond, the most sanguine expectations of its founders and early supporters. For the purpose of awakening and strengthening this feeling of gratitude, we called attention to the simple historical fact that the cry for Bibles from the mountains and valleys of my native principality of Wales led, in the providence of God, to the formation of a society which should supply the land which gave it birth, and largely contribute towards the supply of other lands, and all lands, in all languages, as far and as fast as possible.

But we had another Jubilee object—it was to bear a renewed public testimony to the Divine character and claims of the Bible, and to the right of every individual of the human family to possess it, and to read it in his own vulgar tongue. From a thousand pulpits and platforms, the threefold truth was uttered with no uncertain sound, "The Bible is *from* God; the Bible is *for* man; the Bible is *sufficient*." Subsequent events proved that this part of our Jubilee programme was most providential; for when the enemy came in upon us, from a quarter and in a form least expected, the long and loud Jubilee testimony still reverberated in the ears and thrilled in the hearts of multitudes of our people. The sermons and speeches delivered at this time, the numberless jubilee papers scattered broadcast throughout the length and breadth of the land, and it is but just that I should add, "the Book and its Story," also did good service at this important crisis.

What did Jannes and Jambres gain by withstanding Moses in old times, and what has been gained by their imitators in our day? Let them say what they will, the people who read Holy Scripture in an humble and prayerful spirit have said, and still say, "*Moses is right*"—right in his history, right in his chronology, right in his genealogy, aye, and right in his geology. The people, the multitudes of Christian people, do not hesitate to go a little further, and say with one breath, "*Moses is right, and Colenso is wrong*." Yes, sir, we feel assured that the Bible will outlive this renewed attack, unscathed by the arrows of sarcasm and the shafts of infidelity; uninjured by the severest ordeal of honest criticism; benefited by the discoveries of modern science; confirmed in its statements by the testimony of the rocks and the stones, which are crying out in that land rendered so sacred by its glorious narratives and events.

I am persuaded that after attending the Jubilee meetings so generally held, and reading the books and papers prepared for the occasion, many persons, being enlightened and reassured, were ready to say or sing:

> "Should all the forms that men devise
> Assail my faith with treacherous art,
> I'll call them vanity and lies,
> And bind the Gospel to my heart."

But we had in England, as you also have, a third Jubilee object. We did not *confine* ourselves to thanksgiving to God and testimony in behalf of the good old Book, for we thought it was the right time to give an opportunity to all who were Bible lovers to become Bible givers. We told them that we intended by new and vigorous measures to effect a wide circulation of the Scriptures both at home and abroad. The people generally entered heartily into the Jubilee celebration. The pulpit, the platform, and the press greatly helped us. While the warm heart throbbed with love, and the opened lips sent forth songs of praise, the open hand placed liberal thank-offerings on the Jubilee altar. Never was there a more striking illustration of the well-known lines:

> "What great results from small beginnings spring!"

The very first contribution received towards the Jubilee fund was an old guinea sent me by post by a widow lady living near London. It was on this golden foundation that a noble edifice was raised; around this small coin a large heap was gathered, amounting in the whole to upwards of £110,000 sterling, and exceeding, considerably exceeding, half a million of your dollars, and all this without any diminution in the ordinary annual receipts of the society.

As you may suppose, the possession of so large a sum involved a heavy responsibility, and the committee besought the Lord's help and guidance, so as to be able to spend this money properly and profitably for the good of men, and the glory of Him who redeemed us, not with corruptible things, such as silver and gold, but with his own precious blood.

Relying then upon the Lord for his guidance and blessing, we hastened to convert our Jubilee gold into that which is "better than gold, yea, than much fine gold," and to adopt such special measures as seemed necessary to carry out our practical objects. Special deputations were sent to the British provinces of North America, and the colonies of Australia. New agencies were established or projected with a view to extend the circulation of the Scriptures in various foreign countries. India and Ceylon largely shared in our liberality; and as the Million Testament scheme dovetailed into our Jubilee work, the immense empire of China became an important field of labour. The continent of Europe, more especially Holland, Belgium, and Germany, received large grants of the Sacred Volume. Ireland, always treated as a part of ourselves, received a considerable share of attention, and the grants of Jubilee Bibles and Testaments to societies and schools involved an expenditure of many thousands of pounds. Nor were the claims of home neglected. *Colportage* was established in rural districts, and in crowded manufacturing cities and towns; thus supplying by a new agency the valuable services of our auxiliary societies, and to meet the wants of those who could not be reached by the existing plans of operation. Various city and town missions, with all kinds of benevolent, educational, and religious societies, largely participated in the benefits of the Jubilee fund. It seemed to be the right time to make special grants to hotels, boarding houses, asylums, hospitals, infirmaries, railway and police stations, and the union houses, for the use of the inmates. Nor should I omit to state that advantage was taken of the willingness of the people to contribute to originate a *Benevolent* Fund, with a view to administer in some degree, when circumstances demand it, to the relief and comfort of such as have become old or disabled in the service of the society.

It may be added, and I do it with peculiar satisfaction, that it was during the Jubilee season that other and special modes of circulating the Scriptures amongst the very poorest classes were originated. Who has not heard of the "Bible women" of London? This work also may be regarded as a fruitful offshoot of our great Jubilee tree. It was in the spirit of the Jubilee that a lady well known in Bible society circles as L. N. R., the author of the "Book and its Story," originated a system which she has well described as the "Missing Link" in the chain of Christian benevolence—a system which has worked admirably, and is still carried on most efficiently in the metropolis of England, under her able superintendence.

I have already remarked that the Jubilee year gave an impetus to our work which is still felt. It is a gratifying fact that the yearly receipts and expenditure, and the annual issues of the Sacred Volume, have been gradually but steadily increasing ever since that memorable year. A week ago our anniversary was held at Exeter Hall; and at that great meeting it was the pleasing duty of the secretary to report that the total receipts of the year had amounted to £171,375 10*s.* 2*d.*, and the distribution to 2,296,130 copies of the Sacred Volume; bringing up the grand total to 50,285,709 Bibles and Testaments, or integral portions, in upwards of 170 of the world's languages and dialects.

Before I proceed further, let me say that it affords me the greatest pleasure to find that my countrymen spread over the "States" are amongst the most liberal supporters of the Bible Society. They have been trained to it in the old country, and they carry with them to this land their old Bible society love, and hence the establishment of fifty-seven Welsh branch societies in different parts of this great country. I hope to be able to visit many of these before I return home, and to address the people in their own language—a language which they love, and which I also love as much as any of them. It will afford me the greatest delight to remind them of our well-known Bible society motto, "Bibl i bawb o bobl y byd;" which being interpreted means, a Bible for all the people of the world.

And now, what shall I say in conclusion? Although the British and

Foreign Bible Society may claim precedence in point of age, extent of labour, and amount of expenditure, you may feel assured that we look with no jealous eye upon the efforts of other societies having the same or similar objects in view, but on the contrary, we rejoice in their success, and may it please God to bless them a thousand-fold! But there are special reasons why we should sympathize with the American Bible Society. Had I addressed you some years ago, I might have called you a child of our own; but now that you have reached the respectable age of fifty, we shall regard each other as sisters—affectionate and beloved sisters in the great and honourable though not very ancient Bible society family.

And at the present time—when both societies have grown great, when their ability to do good is rapidly increasing, when facilities for widely extended operations are multiplying on every side, when from many a distant Macedonia the cry is heard, "Come over and help us!" addressed perhaps to both societies simultaneously—what shall I say? Shall I take up the language of Abram to Lot, "Let there be no strife between me and thee, between my herdmen and thy herdmen; for we be brethren?" The world is before us; there remaineth yet very much land to be possessed. Is not the land of promise Immanuel's land? In his name, therefore, and in his strength, let us go up and possess it.

It is my heart's desire that the star-spangled banner of the United States of America and the old union jack of the United Kingdom of Great Britain and Ireland may henceforth wave together on the world's ramparts—recognised every where as symbols of all that is noble in enterprise, honourable in commerce, just in legislation, powerful in union, and sacred in religion.

More than all, it is my prayer to God that these two great Societies, the greatest Bible societies in the world, may always proceed hand in hand, and work side by side, adding translation unto translation, sending forth edition after edition of God's holy Word, and thereby become the instruments of spreading the blessings of peace, and truth, and freedom, and holiness, and happiness, to earth's remotest bounds.

One word more, and I have done. In the review of past success, in the enjoyment of present prosperity, and in the prospect of still greater achievements, we will not forget to say: "Not unto us, O Lord, not unto the British and Foreign; not unto the American Bible Society; not unto any individual man, or set of men; not unto our Charles, or Hughes, or Steinkopff, or Owen, or Wilberforce, or Teignmouth, or Bexley, or Shaftesbury; not unto your Boudinot, or Mason, or Jay, or Bradish, or Frelinghuysen, or Lenox; not unto any of these, or all these put together, but unto the Divine name be all the praise. "For thine is the kingdom, the power, and the glory, for ever and ever." And let all the Christian people on both sides the Atlantic say, Amen, and Amen.

The Rev. Thomas Nolan, B. D., the other delegate from England, a minister of the Episcopal Church in London, then rose, and spoke nearly as follows:

Mr. President: The terms of the resolution you have just heard, the welcome to your Jubilee that it offers, the "warm hearts" and cordial greetings that it mentions, must needs awaken deep emotions within the breasts of those who are embraced within its range; and you may be sure we will "communicate to our several societies your assurance of Christian fellowship and international efforts to send abroad the Bible for the healing of the nations." And yet, when I consider the grandeur of the occasion and the momentousness of the interests that have brought us together to-day from the uttermost parts of the earth, to be present at your Jubilee and to take part in its proceedings, I feel that any allusion merely personal must be altogether beneath the dignity of that occasion and the greatness of those interests. Still, I cannot but recall the thrill of association than ran through me when the proposal was first made to me to undertake a part in this honourable and onerous mission. The prominence of American affairs for the last few years more especially, the portion they must occupy of the world's history for that period, and the influence they must exercise upon its destiny, have directed public attention to them with an intensity, and have drawn out your national characteristics into a boldness of relief, that might have been wanting under ordinary circumstances.

Your interminable territory, your teeming population, your limitless resources, that astonishing resiliency of character, whereby you rise at once above disaster, and regain, as it were, with a bound, even more than your former elevation—these all evoke feelings of overwhelming intensity, before which the prospects of other countries pale in their lustre, and their pigmy proportions are dwarfed into comparative littleness. But when, beside all this, you are enabled to add, as the present occasion invites us to do, an acknowledgment of God in all his ways, with the encouraging assurance that He will direct your paths, then the picture is complete. That which was grand becomes enduring also; that which was full of hope for the country to which it belongs appears likewise fraught with the seeds of blessing to the nations of the earth, and of peace to the family of man. Truly the associations and suggestions of such a meeting as this are among the most sublime and inspiriting of which the human mind and heart are capable. That feeling is acknowledged; its spirit is evidently shed abroad; its influence is felt. I believe and am sure that a blessing is with us.

It has been our lot in England, during the last twenty years, to celebrate the jubilee of more than one of our great religious societies, and it seems natural upon such occasions to go back to their first origin, and all the more because of its calling up the names of the great and the good who have passed away from us, who have, however, bequeathed to us their example, and thus, though dead, still speak. My colleague, Dr. Phillips, has already mentioned some honoured names in connexion with our British and Foreign Bible Society; and on Sunday evening last, when it was my privilege to hear the reverend and learned Chancellor Ferris, of your University, on this subject, he too unfurled the roll of worthies that belong to your own American Bible Society, and did honour to the mighty dead, as he recalled their names and recorded their services. In particular (and I am reminded of it by the manner in which my dear and right reverend friend Bishop M'Ilvaine has borne testimony also to the only survivor from 1816 now present) did Dr. Ferris, with a voice trembling from emotion, and in terms touching and tender, that did honour to his own heart also, bear witness to the lifelong services of his friend and pastor, the venerable Dr. Gardiner Spring.

In reviewing the early struggles and the matured success of great works of this kind, one must be struck with the hand of God, made manifest upon occasions with Divine interpositions, for they are nothing less, without which they could not, humanly speaking, have held on their way or accomplished their object. Such, for example, was the discovery of stereotype printing, that preceded by a little the formation of the British and Foreign Bible Society in 1804. By means of this discovery two objects were rendered feasible, without which the work of Bible circulation would have been all but impossible; I mean the power of multiplying copies and of reducing the cost of publication. Is not this Jubilee similarly signalized? and shall we not acknowledge the same merciful hand as the bestower of the gift? The superb appliances that belong to your magnificent Bible House are at this moment busily employed, under the experienced and accomplished guidance of Dr. Van Dyck, in electrotyping a copy of the Arabic Scriptures. And the indispensable importance of this application of science to this purpose—a result as much in advance of the ordinary stereotyping as that was in advance of any thing that had gone before—will be obvious from the fact stated by Dr. Van Dyck, that with all the appliances available at Beirut and Smyrna, it would take six thousand years to place a copy of the Arabic Scriptures in the hands of each of the one hundred and twenty millions of human beings, who are accessible through no other channel; and that even with all the advantages of electrotyping now at work, it will require six hundred years to do the same. But you are rising to the greatness of the Macedonian cry sent forth to you. There is work for all the presses that can be set to work to hurry on such a desirable consummation. And this American Bible Society has most cordially acceded to the request of the committee in London, and will make for them duplicate electrotype plates of such editions of the Arabic Scriptures now in course of preparation as they may designate, without charge, the only stipulation being that no alterations be made in the plates without the assent of the American Bible Society. To this the committee in London returned the following reply, which it is my delight as well as my duty to read to this meeting:

Resolved, That the committee have received with peculiar satisfaction the noble offer of the American Bible Society to present to this society, free of charge, duplicate electrotype plates of such editions of the Arabic translation of the Scriptures, prepared by the Rev. Dr. Van Dyck, as the committee may select from the series which it is intended to issue in connexion with the Jubilee of the American Bible Society; and the committee, while accepting the liberal proposal, desire heartily to reciprocate the kind and Christian sentiments by which it has been dictated, and to convey to the Board of the American Bible Society the assurance of their warmest gratitude for the generosity evinced in regard to the work in question, and trust that the transaction, so honourable to those with whom it originates, may tend to strengthen the many friendly ties which unite the two Societies in their great enterprise of Scripture circulation throughout the world.

Surely, sir, it is a token for good that these two great Boards in America and in England are animated with this feeling of mutual respect and generous confidence towards each other? Is it not from Him who causeth men, and boards, and nations, to be of one mind?

If time allowed, it would be both interesting and instructive to trace the hand and favour of God similarly manifested in the events that were overruled at the period of the Reformation for the furtherance of his purpose and the spread of his Word. The discovery of printing by Gutenberg and Schœffer, of the mariner's compass, and of the great continent of America in 1492, were all subsidiary to the great purposes of God, and intensified the power and preciousness of the Reformation. We might go back also to the rise of Christianity itself, and we might in the triumphs of Alexander the Great find an unconscious preparation for the great event that was impending. The Ptolemies, the Alexandrian library, the Septuagint translation of the Old Testament Scriptures, the ascendency of the Greek language and literature at the time, were all overruled as disciplining the mind of man for what was about to take place, and prepared many beforehand to receive the tidings of "a Saviour, Christ the Lord." Is it too much to say that there was a previous training of the children of Israel, during their long bondage in Egypt, for the great work for which God designed them? "Ye are my witnesses, saith the Lord;" "this people have I formed for myself; they shall shew forth my praise." And is it not of God also, this concurrence of many things with this your year of Jubilee, which seems to place an open door before you, and to bid you to enter upon it? Is it not of God that the blessings of peace and union should have been restored to you, just as your Jubilee was completed—that the South should be opened to your Christian efforts, and Ethiopia, as it were, stretching out her hands to you for the Word of God? You have already proved yourselves capable of rising to any emergency. You leave a glorious past behind you, only to enter upon the still more glorious future that, by God's blessing, awaits and invites you.

It is hard to pass by the many aspects of this "holy and beautiful" work that might well demand a notice; but the number of the speakers and the convenience of the meeting render it impossible. I should like to have remarked upon the noble catholicity of your constitution, as well as of our own, that has been tested by the experience of more than half a century, and that has gone far to realize the fond aspiration of Lord Bexley many years ago, when he said in reply to some opponent, "If we cannot reconcile all opinions, let us endeavour to unite all hearts." I should like to have dwelt for a little upon the nobleness of the simple object aimed at by both Societies, that the "Word of the Lord should have free course and be glorified." Oh, sir, what is there that in any degree so contributes to the glory of God, or to the benefit and blessings of the human race? "The entrance of God's Word giveth light." Sanctification is by the truth. His Word is truth. It is able to make wise unto salvation. It is profitable for every thing—that the man of God may be perfect, thoroughly furnished unto all good works. If one of the great orators of antiquity still stirs our hearts with his matchless appeal on behalf of science and polite literature, beginning with, "Hœc studia juventutem alunt, senectutem oblectant," etc.—I won't trouble you with the quotation—how much more are the Scriptures of truth, God's revealed will and inspired Word, deserving of such commendation! "When thou goest, it shall lead thee; when thou sleepest, it shall keep thee; and when thou awakest, it shall talk with thee." The Hon. Mr. Winthrop has told us that we might part with Shakspeare from our literature, or even with Homer from antiquity; but he is not prepared to give up a book, a chapter, or even a verse of God's blessed Word. Oh, no, sir! to deprive us of that, or to weaken our full confidence in it, would be to rob the young man of his guide, the matured man of his companion, the rich man of his counsellor, the poor man of his stay, the old man of his consolation, and the dying man of his hope. Oh, my friends, bind it for ever to your own souls; prize it more and more, in your closets, in your families, in your churches; lose no opportunity of extending it to, and of sharing it with others; and in so doing you will multiply its abundance and enhance its preciousness to yourselves. All the blessings you possess are contemporaneous with your possession of the Word of God, and their continuance with you depends upon the extent to which you cherish and obey it.

Every good gift and every perfect gift is from God; and the title, as it were, by which we hold it is the honour we do to his Word. In this land, where liberty is so valued and freedom is cherished, as it is in my own, let it never be forgotten that every kind of freedom comes from, and is strengthened by, the free use of the Word of God. Neither your social, your intellectual, or your political freedom were worth a year's purchase unless in connexion with spiritual freedom first. Political freedom is the own child of religious freedom. Look back to the Reformation. Was not the experiment then tried and the principle established? Europe then was a vast prison house, of which the key was at Rome, and the jailor the accomplished Leo X. But the Bible was emancipated; the great prisoners went forth—apostles, prophets, and evangelists. Luther gave free course to the Word of God, and the tribes of Germany were enabled to hear, in their own tongue in which they were born, the wonderful works of God. The Reformation was won, and the foundation was therein laid for all the triumphs that freedom hath ever since achieved. But you will observe the order and the connexion. Religious freedom first, then the others followed in her train. Religious freedom awoke first, as it were, from the long trance of the dark ages; she aroused her slumbering sister and bade her follow in the resurrection.

Was it not something of the same that took place in England towards the close of the last century? When the church missionary, and the religious tract, and the British and Foreign Bible Societies were called into existence, darkness might be said to have covered the earth, and gross darkness the people; when God mercifully interposed again, and rolled back the clouds, and said, as it were, "Let there be light; and there was light"—even "the light of the knowledge of the glory of God in the face of Jesus Christ." Oh yes, sir, Jesus Christ is the "All in all" of the Bible: it is his finished work, redemption completed in his blood, that makes the Bible precious. The spirit of it all is the testimony of Jesus. To you that believe it He is precious. This is what Dr. Chalmers called the "portable evidence" to the truth of God, or what a greater than Chalmers called the witness of God's Spirit "bearing witness with our spirit, that we are the children of God." Oh, I beseech you, rest not satisfied with any thing till you have arrived at this—the "Spirit of adoption, whereby we cry Abba, Father."

This is a glorious and inviting theme, and boundless is the prospect that it opens before us. But I must deny myself, and come in conclusion to the object for which I have been delegated here—to acknowledge the welcome with which you have introduced us to this great meeting, and to discharge, "pro virili mea," the commission with which I and my colleague have been charged—to express to the American Bible Society the heartiest congratulations of the committee at home upon this auspicious occasion; and to assure them of the high and unalloyed respect that they entertain towards them, as well as of the deep sympathy and the congenial interest that is felt in all their difficulties and in all their successes. A community of object and an identity of means, in a case like ours, are the most reliable grounds of mutual respect and lasting friendship; and in this matter nothing can be nearer nor closer than ours. We serve the same Master, we rely upon the same blessing, we are met by the same difficulties, we look for the same reward; and this over a field so wide that it renders rivalry impossible, except that holy one, as to who shall love the Saviour most and serve Him best.

I was invited to attend a meeting of our committee, held on the Monday before I left home; all was conducted in the same manner and spirit that characterized the proceedings of your own Board on Thursday last, when I had the honour to be present. All was sanctified, as with yourselves, by the Word of God and by prayer. When they commended my colleague and myself to God for our journey and our mission, every expression was full of brotherly love, of sympathy and joy, rejoicing in your joy, and giving God praise and thanksgiving for his goodness to you; and you may rest assured that it will be our delight, no less than our duty, faithfully to report, on our return, the cordial and generous response on your part with which their greetings were met, as well as our debt immense of personal kindness to ourselves.

Why should it not be so? Why should any root of bitterness be allowed to spring up to mar the harmony that ought to subsist between the two committees, societies, nations? Sir, the man that would foment discord between us is not the friend of either, but the enemy of both. I do believe that the hearts of the two countries are, in the main, right with each other. Great occasions, suddenly arising, stir up the very depths of the soul, and expose what lay concealed there. When the dreadful news of the assassination of President Lincoln reached us, at which humanity stood aghast, and freedom turned pale, the heart of England was appalled and trembled as instinctively as of America herself. Even small occasions also afford reliable indications of popular feeling, as the floating straw shows the direction of the mighty current. When one of your war steamers—I can't pronounce the name—put into Belfast last month, the commander and officers were received, as they should be, by the mayor of that great city, the New York of Ireland. I remember the toast at the banquet, to which your officers were called upon to respond—"Unbroken friendship between the United Kingdom and the United States." When I read that in London, I was so much pleased with it, that I put it down in my commonplace book, little imagining that such an opportunity as the present would be afforded me of referring to it. Again, it was my good fortune to make the acquaintance, on my voyage out, of that eminent philanthropist, your distinguished countryman, George Peabody, Esq. He showed me the autograph letter of the Queen of England, in acknowledgment of his munificent and unparalleled liberality to the poor of the metropolis—a liberality that, if report be true, he is about to repeat in the loved land of his birth. Our noble queen admired him all the more for the tenacity with which he adhered to his citizenship of the United States, for which he respectfully declined the highest honour that her majesty was willing to confer upon him. In his reply he gracefully expressed the high value he set upon the letter, as testifying to "the kindly feeling between the Queen of the United Kingdom and a citizen of the United States." Another instance occurs to me that I cannot forbear to mention: Ten or twelve years ago, when his Excellency the lamented Abbott Lawrence was your Representative at the Court of St. James, I had the honour to meet him at the annual breakfast of the Young Men's Christian Association, held at a quarter before six o'clock in the morning, over which the Earl of Harrowby presided. His excellency, in addressing the young men, remarked, talking of his own country, that America and England united in friendship might defy the world. Suddenly pausing, he added: "No, I recall the word 'defy;' this is no occasion of defiance; but rather let me wish that England and America, united upon the basis of the Bible, may become a blessing to the world."

One word more, and I trespass no longer upon this most indulgent meeting. By an undesigned coincidence, this day of your Jubilee celebration is Ascension Day—fraught with hopes and associations most precious to the Christian heart, and always observed in the Christian Church. Upon this day the top-stone was placed, as it were, upon the work of redemption, as far as it has been perfected hitherto. By the incarnation He took manhood into God, and capacitated himself for death. By death He destroyed him that had the power of death, that is, the devil. By the resurrection He "declared himself to be the Son of God with power." By his ascension, He took his place at the right hand of the Father, to wait until his enemies should be made his footstool. Upon this part of his purpose He is pausing still; but God's longsuffering is salvation may we not add, in a certain sense, and that through us? Great privileges, in connexion with great opportunities, always bring with them tremendous responsibilities. America and England are placed in the forefront of the battle. God grant they may both be found faithful to their high trust! England's prosperity and England's religion have always advanced hand in hand together. It cannot be otherwise with America. The fondest wish of my heart for both may be expressed in words familiar to most of us—that "peace and happiness, truth and justice, religion and piety, may be established in both for all generations."

In the absence of full reports of the addresses of Drs. Taylor and Ormiston of Canada, we take the following brief notice from the columns of the New York Observer:

Rev. LACHLIN TAYLOR, of Canada, after a pleasing reference to the previous speakers, conveyed Canadian salutations. He regarded this as a providential occasion in the political and national history, for the Jubilee celebration of a Society that scatters "the Book" broadcast over all the world. In the Jewish year of jubilee the trump of freedom sounded for all, and it was fitting that the emancipation of millions and this celebration should occur together. He offered a sincere and poetical tribute to the memory of President Lincoln, and, after a brief speech, gave way to the Rev. Dr. ORMISTON, of Canada, who heartily concurred in the expressions of sympathy and congratulation which had been offered by the other delegates; and as he first saw the light in the land of the mountain and the flood, of the heather and the broom, where he first learned at a mother's knee to read the Bible, and where he learned from it the way of salvation through Jesus Christ, he would bring also a voice of greeting and good will from the banks of the Clyde as well as from Canada. The Bible cause is commended by its catholicity to all; its work is to give the Holy Word to every human being. God has given resources of mind and material enough to give the Bible to every creature within the next fifty years. Has God created mouths for which He has not created food? And has He not created material enough and mind, that, inspired by Him, shall develope this material for the multiplying and spreading of his Holy Word? Is it said that there are not agencies enough to do this work? Agencies! why, what are all our congregations about? Poor, withered, rusting souls, all through the land, are literally dying for want of something to do. As he came to this city a year ago, he stopped at the house of an aged woman who long years ago found her Saviour in the blessed Bible; and having found Him, she at once asked what she could do for Him. It seemed natural that, as the Bible had led her to

Christ, she should devote her energies to spreading the Bible. And from that day she had devoted all that she could spare from the labour of her hands to send Bibles to others; and he saw the channel worn in her aged hands by the needle, which ceased not to ply while she told him of her love and work for Christ, and that by God's help she had been able thus to earn $1,000 for the Bible cause. And this same woman, during one year, earned a Bible a day—365 copies during the year, by her consecrated industry. Dr. Ormiston made most telling and practical application of this and other facts to the Marys and Marthas in the assembly, urging all to distinguish this Jubilee year by personal effort. The audience united in singing, "The year of Jubilee is come."

Rev. Cesar Pascal, delegate from the Bible Society of France, said:

Christian Friends: When I ask myself what entitles me to represent at this great Jubilee gathering the Bible Society of France, I find no other title to this flattering distinction but my sympathy with the Biblical work and the noble and glorious republic of the United States. It would have been easy for my brethren in France to find a delegate more authorized by age, talents, or services rendered, but it was impossible for them to send you a more sincere friend. I will even say that by selecting me they have found the man in whom are embodied the feelings of fraternity and devotedness they have ever cherished toward you. Hence I have not hesitated to accept the important and distant mission offered me, assured as I was, by sympathetic presentiments, that you would receive me with a cordiality equal to that which I was to bring in your midst.

And now, American brethren, I am happy to meet you under these pleasant and solemn circumstances. I gladly stand before you to offer you the tribute of sympathy, of gratitude, and of congratulation, which the "Bible Society of France" has commissioned me to bring you from across the waters.

You have extended to it a fraternal invitation to take part in these Jubilee exercises, and it has hastened to choose a representative who would mingle his thanksgivings with yours, and his petitions with those you address to heaven for the prosperity of your country and your Society. For we, too, evangelical Christians of France, are thankful to God for the signal protection He has ever vouchsafed to America, and particularly for the happy issue to which He has brought the long and terrible crisis through which you have just passed with a devotedness, a courage, and a firmness which have justly earned for you the admiration of the civilized world. And why should not our hearts be filled with gratitude as well as yours? What God has caused to triumph on this new continent is not simply the cause of the United States, but that of humanity itself—the holy cause of liberty and justice, for which you have had the triple glory of struggling, of suffering, and overcoming. Nor have the Protestant churches of France ever offered so many fervent prayers for you as during the past five years. Your great trial has revealed to them the strength of the bonds of sympathy which unite them to you; and the proofs they have given you of their lively interest have been so diverse and so expressive, that we can say in truth that they have morally shared your vicissitudes—your sadness, your mourning, your tears, as well as your gratitude, your joys, and your thanksgivings.

To these feelings which you have called forth as a nation, and which are common to all Protestants in France, the Bible Society of France adds affectionate feelings of Christian brotherhood toward the American Bible Society; for the two Societies are bound together by those sweet and powerful ties which spring out of a perfect oneness of faith, of spirit, and end. Our Bible Society is, like yours, founded upon a belief in the inspiration of the Holy Scriptures, which i recognises and proclaims as the infallible and sovereign rule of doctrine and life. Like your Society, ours labours with a truly liberal spirit; rising above ecclesiastical differences, it admits among its members indiscriminately the faithful of any evangelical denomination, and distributes to all the *Word of Life;* to those of Independent, Wesleyan, Baptist, and Lutheran churches, as well as those of the venerable French Reformed Church. Finally, like your Society, its aim is to place the Bible in every family, that it may be as a domestic altar, sanctifying the trials and joys of home; and to scatter the Sacred Sheet wherever the Lord shall present an open door and furnish the means.

From this *ensemble* of similarity and fraternal relations results, for the Bible Society of France, that sympathy, already of long date and deep, which it cherishes for you, and of which my presence among you must be a certain pledge. Hence you will not wonder that our society has seen with a joy that can be equalled only by yours, the enlarging from year to year of the means and the influence of your powerful Association, which numbers already by millions the sacred volumes it has distributed. We remember with emotion the beautiful spectacle your Society offered during the years of fratricidal struggle which still saddens many hearts. Whilst such a variety of interests suffered; whilst the financial crisis weighed heavily upon all citizens, and the national debt ceased to be computed by millions, the American Bible Society had means in such abundance that it increased its operations, established new and numerous auxiliaries, and enlarged by thousands its circulation of the Scriptures. Ah! you are right, dear brethren, in saying that the smile of God has been upon your work as well as your country. The protection of the Almighty has kept pace with your difficulties; so that, far from hiding it from human view, perils have only made it the more striking. You have understood, honoured friends, that such blessings imposed upon you the duty of greater efforts, more zeal and activity; and with joy and unanimity you have resolved to consecrate yourselves more fully and generally to your great task, so that no part of it could be neglected. Your rich country invites evermore the children of men, without distinction of race or nationality, to share its abundance. To all those who, through the holy path of labour, seek to reach a better condition, it offers precious resources, whose efficacy is certain with the blessing of God. This is what your Society aims to do for the eternal treasures of which the Bible is the inexhaustible mine. It will offer to all, without exception, the precious means of securing a moral and spiritual condition better already in this world, and in the world to come a place in the eternal habitations. This is, brethren, fulfilling at once the duties of the Christian and the citizen, and this country must be grateful to your Society for all it will do in this direction. For if there is a well-established fact in the history of the United States, it is, that to the Bible the country owes its powerful institutions, its fruitful liberty, which excites the jealousy of many nations, its wonderful prosperity, and its numerous works of evangelization and benevolence. The Bible has given it its prominent place in the world. It is with reason, American friends, that you consider your fidelity to the Word of God as the safeguard of all your liberties, and the source of all your prosperity. If ever (forbid it, God!) this Bible, which it is your mission to give to the whole world, were taken away from you, and human traditions of any kind were substituted in its place, I assert, with all the authority which history gives me, it would be the downfall of the greatness of the United States. They would decline by degrees, and their decay, though perhaps slow, would be none the less sure and deep. Looked at from this high standpoint, the destinies of your country rest to a great e tent, under God, with societies like this. How noble is your task; but how heavy your responsibility! May God, without whose blessing all efforts are powerless, give you to rise more and more to the height of your mission! May your country and your Bible Society continue to enjoy his favour, and may both be led to the high destinies He has in store for them!

The Rev. Isaac G. Bliss, of Constantinople, offered the following:

Resolved, That we celebrate this Jubilee with gratitude to God for his favour in the past, with hope for the future, with love for all who love his Word, and with enlarged purposes for its wider circulation.

Mr. President: I am most happy to move this resolution, for I am confident that the heart of each person responds most joyfully to the sentiments it contains. The Jews of old hallowed the fiftieth year, and caused the trumpet of jubilee to be sounded throughout the land. I think, sir, that the Treasurer would have been sustained by this Society if he had authorized me to bring from Egypt or Judea a genuine ram's horn trumpet, with which to sound forth our praise to God and our gratitude for the success with which He has crowned the past efforts of this Society, both at home and abroad. But, sir, without ram's horn or trumpet, we will praise the Lord for his mighty acts; we will praise Him for his excellent greatness. The resolution says that we celebrate this Jubilee with hope for the future. Every day the work spreads, and the Master is true to his promise. But we say we celebrate this Jubilee with love for all who love his Word. Yes, sir, with love for all who love his Word, of every family, of every sect, of every nation, of every kindred, on the face of all the earth; for love is the fulfilment of the law. The resolution so says that we celebrate this Jubilee with enlarged purposes, for the wider circulation of the Word of God. Yes, sir; with these purposes, every one of them riveted in the centre of each heart, we propose to control all love, all ambition; to control all selfishness, that we may not fail to accomplish just that which our Master wishes us to accomplish, not only in this good native land of ours, but in all the earth.

I cannot but feel honoured with the position assigned me as the representative of the American Bible Society in the Levant—an area of more than 1,200,000 square miles, and equal to the United States of America, exclusive of the territories. It contains a population of more than 50,000,000, made up of ten distinct classes, or I may say races of men, using a variety of languages and dialects, which I presume can be found in no other portion of the world. Is it not strange, sir, that the land where was the first home of our race, where was our earliest civilization, where our Saviour lived and died, where the Bible originated, is at this day, in this eighteenth century, so destitute of the Word of God? There have not been circulated as yet, in all that broad land, half a million copies of the Scriptures. Within the past eight years, during which I have been the representative of this Society in the Levant, we have been permitted by this Society, in conjunction with the British and Foreign Bible Society of England, to put into circulation by sale, at fully one third the cost, nearly 200,000 copies. Sir, the American Bible Society have gone through all the length and breadth of that land, opening there 71,000 Bibles; the rest belong to our fund across the ocean. We have received into the treasury of New York, through my hands, more than $22,000, and more than $28,000 have gone to the treasury in London, making in all more than $51,000 contributed by the people of Turkey—the poor, downtrodden people of Turkey—for the Bibles they have received. The number of copies of the Scripture thus paid for in Turkey go right where they are designed to go. If you can get ten piasters out of a Turk for a pocket Testament, if you can get any thing for a Bible, it makes sure that that Bible will be read, and that it will be the means of the salvation, if not of the man receiving it, at least of some one connected with him.

Now, sir, we have put these 200.000 copies of the Scriptures and its parts into circulation, and in the face of an opposition which you can hardly understand. I might show you in detail what this opposition arrayed against us is; but at this time I will only ask you to call to mind what Turkey is; what Mohammedan intolerance and exclusiveness is; what the religion of Islam implies, and then tell you there are 21,000,000 of Mohammedans in Turkey—an empire the very laws and purpose of which are to suppress, if possible, the religion of Jesus Christ. Against these Mohammedans there are arrayed 15,000,000 of corrupt nominal Christians, possessed of a half heathen civilization, and making use of the rites and ceremonies of a half heathen religion. There are monasteries by the hundred and cloisters by the thousand, all of which are watching with a spirit of the intensest anxiety any feeling of uneasiness on the part of the people. Notwithstanding all this opposition, we have done a good work in getting so many copies of the Scriptures into the hands of the people. There, in the great, wicked city of Constantinople, we have sold 4,775 copies of the Scriptures, and have received therefor $3,000. The hungering and thirsting for the Scriptures which is found in some parts of Turkey is repressed by the cloisters wherever repression is possible; yet in one of the provinces, in the course of eight years, more than 8,000 copies of the Scriptures have been sold to poor people—to very poor people.

Now, I presume you would all like to hear some stories. We are now in Turkey, but will go into Egypt. We will go half way up the Nile, and there, about twenty miles distant from the river, you will find a poor woman who has been hard at work, and who walked twenty miles and back, barefoot, in the sands of Egypt, in order to get possession of an Arabic Bible. After having reached the missionary's house, she presented herself, and asked if Bibles were sold there. When told they were, she was asked if she could read. She then took up a New Testament, and being almost blind, put it close up to her eyes. After having read a chapter, she told in her own words what it was about. She then asked if she could not have a Bible. A Bible was given her, and she immediately set out again on her homeward track over the burning sands. Go with me, if you please, into Mesopotamia; I will point you to a man who has recently obtained a Bible. A few years ago he felt in his heart a desire to know something more of the contents of the Bible. There was but one Bible in the village, and that was in the ancient Armenian language. He went to the man who owned it, and offered the entire avails of his silk crop for it, and was refused. I don't suppose that the value of his silk crop would compare with some of the incomes of this city, but it was all he had. The man said, "I must have a Bible; I will go to Jerusalem." On his way thither he came to a city called Cesarea, where he found a Bible in the ancient Armenian language, which was offered him for three hundred and fifty piasters, or about fourteen dollars. But thinking that he might find one cheaper, he declined to take it. He reached at length a town near the place where Paul was born, and found a copy of an Armenian Bible for eight hundred piasters, or thirty-seven dollars. He hesitated whether to take it or not, but finally determined to go to Jerusalem. When he arrived there, he could not find a single copy of the Word of God; but he did find a few tracts designed to show that the religion of the Bible was a false religion. As he could not get a Bible, he was persuaded to take some three or four of these tracts. He returned home. On his way back, he intended to stop and obtain the worn and torn Bible that had been offered to him for three hundred and fifty piasters; but before he could get there he was taken sick, and he soon had no money with which to buy that Bible, and so he went home to his native village. After reaching home he went to see a neighbour, who had a large reference Armenian Bible, published by this Society. When the owner of the Bible was asked how much he gave for it, his reply was, "Forty piasters; that a colporteur of a Bible Society had sold it to him, and that he would be along again before many months." "Oh," said the man who had been to Jerusalem, "they asked me eight hundred piasters for one not half so good as this, and this is in a language that I can understand." He took out his tracts. Eight or ten of his neighbours came together to read these tracts. They did not like the spirit of them. They began to compare them with what they found in the Bible. The result was, that those eight or ten men were made to feel that it was the Word of God. They sent a deputation, that they might purchase for eight or ten men as many Bibles as they needed. From that village there has gone out over the surrounding villages an influence in favour of the truth which you can hardly understand here.

This man was the founder of a Bible society, the like of which is not to be found in all Turkey. They became acquainted with the Bible, and every Sunday they started out, two and two, with their Bibles in their hands, to read to the people in the villages near by. In all those villages we have found on examination that there are a large number of Bible readers.

Let me now take you to the region of Ararat. I have long tried to find some person who would go as a colporteur into that region. During the last winter we found two men, who started away with their packages of Bibles on their backs. In some of the villages they sold seventeen copies of the Bible, where no one would have supposed that they could sell a single one. They were driven out of one of these villages, one cold stormy night, because they were simply Bible colporteurs. One woman so far relented as to give them a little rice. After they had finished their meals she found out that they were Protestant Bible sellers; she then took the spoon, broke it and threw it into the fire, saying it could not be used again, because it had been used by a Protestant.

A glorious work is being done in Turkey. Now, shall we, or shall we not have a wider circulation of the Bible? It is for you, Mr. President, and for the Board of Managers to answer this question. The preparations are all made for the work. Will you sustain your Agent, and allow him to have all the colporteurs he wants? If so, I shall be exceedingly thankful.

The resolution was seconded by the Rt. Rev. CHARLES P. M'ILVAINE, D.D., of Ohio, who spoke as follows:

I should not have thought of such a thing as undertaking to say a single word in connexion with this resolution, seconding the motion, had it not been particularly requested of me (I say it for the purpose of excusing myself), and the request laid especially upon the ground that in the year 1853, when the British and Foreign Bible Society was celebrating its jubilee, I was one with another venerable and beloved brother, Dr. Vermilye, of this city, who were honoured with the commission of this Society to represent it at that jubilee.

I not only greet those who have been sent here to our Jubilee from England, and from France, and the colonies of Great Britain, but I thank them most heartily, in the name of this great Society, for the cheering words, the affectionate expressions of strong desire of future communion and increasing love wherewith they have come to us. Allusion was made by one of the delegates from England to the mother society, although one of them said that it was perhaps too late to speak of this Society as the daughter. Very well; when questions of right and enterprise come together, we stand together as sisters; but when questions of memory, and origin, and reverence, come before us, then we delight to take the place of the daughter, and say to that beloved and venerated society of England: "Dear mother, dear mother, we own thy parentage; we love to think of the time when thou wert the only great national institution of the whole earth, and when thy example taught us our duty; and we love to feel, and we always have loved to feel, in reverence and thankfulness; and we shall love to follow, counting and knowing it to be a privilege to so follow, in the steps of that venerated parent to the end of the world." Nothing, nothing, American brethren, can we do for the good of the world so much as that we, the two great Protestant nations of the earth, should stand together to the end of the world for the world's work and salvation; and no other instrumentality can be devised so mighty, or so certain of its result to that great end, as keeping together as co-workers, and taking a common interest in the circulating of our common Bible, and especially in our common version. I trust our dear brethren, and especially those from England, will go back and tell them, that just as Dr. Vermilye and myself received such kind greetings at their jubilee, so they received the strongest and warmest exhibitions of kindred love: and I trust that as the shuttle, of which I spoke while in England, and to which allusion has been made, going to and fro, weaving more and more, broader and broader, and stronger and stronger, the golden robe of our Christian union, so ever hereafter, not merely on Jubilee occasions, but from anniversary to anniversary, that work of love, harmony, and union, may go forward. But to change the figure from raiment to telegraphing: Between the two great Protestant nations of the earth, down beneath all the waters of strife, there lies a strong cable of golden love, over which travel messages of kindness, of mutual co-operation, suggestion, and incitement. There was a cable that the art of man laid with great expense of man's means, but it broke.

The theory is with regard to any thing that man may lay down in the deep, that the terrors and strife of the ocean may still interfere with the communication desired. There is, however, a cable laid by God, down so deep that the art and malice of men can never reach; so perfect that nothing can ever add to it; and over it messages of love will be continually passing. God is in it; no waves of human discord can interrupt it. There it is, the strong bond of Christian love between England and us.

The Bishop here narrated at much length the incidents of the first Sabbath which he spent in England in 1861, when the excitement over "the Trent affair" had just begun to surge over that country. He was the first to bring the tidings that "our government had nothing to do with it." In three churches which he visited in London on that day, the object of every sermon preached and of many prayers offered was to keep down excitement, to prevent war or any conflict between the two great nations. In the Baptist chapel in which Gen. Havelock was formerly a worshipper, and where Sir Morton Peto was an elder, the Bishop made his way to the pulpit stairs to respond to the sentiments of the preacher, who said: "Pray for her Majesty, pray for the lords and commons in parliament, pray for the Queen's cabinet, pray for the President of the United States, pray for the Senate and House of Representatives, pray for the Cabinet, pray that peace may be kept, pray that the spirit of war may be kept down in both lands." It being Communion Sunday, and the ordinance of the Lord's Supper being about to be administered, there was no room for the American's response.

The Bishop then proceeded:

In conclusion, there was not a pulpit in all England in which the same sort of work had not gone on in earnest efforts to keep the two countries in peace, and in the manifestation of kind sentiment towards us, except in one instance, and that was in a church in London, where the congregation, supposing that the minister intended to say something of a contrary kind, made such a noise that he had to stop; and he was obliged to come out in the "Times" the next day, and say that he did not mean to utter any such sentiment. There is a great depth of Christian love, a strong feeling of attachment; and I believe that when these winds of passions shall have passed away, we shall be found nearer together than ever before, and there we must be for the good of the whole world.

I want to state what I consider to be the testimony of this meeting—what I consider to be the testimony of every great meeting like this for the circulation of the Scriptures. The two great battles to be fought are, with infidelity growing under the name of rationalism and under the name of popery, each growing with parallel power and rapidity; and which I consider this Society can successfully combat under that single verse of St. Paul to Timothy: "All Scripture is given by inspiration of God, and is profitable for doctrine, for reproof, for correction, for instruction in righteousness; that the man of God may be perfect, thoroughly furnished unto all good works."

Take the first, that all Scripture, every chapter, every verse, is given by the inspiration of God, that inspiration which God can only give. There is our testimony against the whole world of man's philosophy and man's skepticism. The bare fact that we come together from England and every where, and are standing around the solitary Volume, and sending it abroad at such expense and earnestness to the end of the world, is declaration of supernatural inspiration and influence. It is utterly impossible that that zeal should exist in the world, and especially that it should be fruitful of any such results, if in our own estimation we took up with any thing else in the place of God's Inspired Word as the final rule of faith and practice. Let it be in any sense man's work, as distinct from God's Inspired Word, bringing it down from that high level of God's supremacy and sovereignty, and Bible societies dwindle away to nothing, and people will be content that the world shall be without the Bible. Then as to the other part of the verse—that it is "profitable for doctrine, for reproof, for correction, for instruction in righteousness; that the man of God may be perfect, thoroughly furnished unto all good works"—the sufficiency of the Scriptures. Let that which is the great bulwark of popery nominally—necessity of tradition, the necessity of the word of the Church to supplement the Scriptures, to make them sufficient—be the sentiment of Christendom and Bible societies, and the zeal to circulate the single Volume without note or comment is at an end; because we shall not think any thing of the efficacy of that Book's circulation until we gather up the whole load of the tradition of the ages and send them together.

Now, then, when we stand with such zeal to circulate that simple Book, we say it is given by inspiration of God, or we would not care any thing about sending it. If it is such as that the man of God can, by the simple blessing of the Spirit of God upon the teaching of that Word, thoroughly furnish and make a perfect man in Christ Jesus, then we have the perfect sufficiency of the Scriptures.

Therefore let us gather together our testimony; let us carry it away as our united testimony to the perfect inspiration and the perfect sufficiency of God's Holy Word. Then let me just add this: we want something after all to make that Word of God sufficient. Then we go to the precincts of Gethsemane, and we find our blessed Lord praying, "Sanctify them through thy truth; thy word is truth." Well, then, not only do we think that that Word is God's great instrumentality for the sanctification of the world, but that He who is ever living at the right hand of God to make intercession for us is interceding for the efficacy and sufficiency of the Scriptures, of the entire Word of God; and therefore, when we go abroad with the circulation, it is not that we rely upon that Word or any thing that we put with it, but rely, constantly looking up to heaven, and thinking of the intercession of the Son of God at the right hand of the Father; and there we put our trust; such is our hope. It is Jesus beginning, ending, first and last, our dear Saviour, our glorious portion. In his strength we are strong, and by Him the Word is sufficient.

Remarks of Bishop Janes:

The last reverend speaker quoted this passage of Scripture, "That the Scriptures are profitable for instruction;" and one of the instructions of the Bible is, in honour to prefer one another; and I shall on this occasion prefer that the succeeding speaker shall have your time and attention. I have too delicate an appreciation of what is due to those who are to follow, on such an occasion, to encroach on their time. I will simply move the resolution. The resolution will commend itself to your hearty spirit and practice; and I am persuaded that this is the best service I can render to the Cause which has brought us together to-day. The light is not sufficient to enable me to read the resolution.

Resolution read by Dr. TAYLOR, as follows:

Resolved, That, relying upon the providence and grace of the Almighty God, this Society hereby approves the resolutions adopted by the Board of Managers at their last meeting, to undertake without delay a third general supply of the whole country with the Word of God—a work which is eminently befitting us as an acknowledgment of Divine goodness in the past, and a proper beginning of our second half century.

Bishop Janes: I most heartily move that resolution, and yield the opportunity to speak to a man whom we all delight to honour, both for his Christian character and the high services which he has rendered his country.

Remarks of Rev. Dr. VERMILYE:

I was going to say there was little of any thing Bishop Janes could produce I could not second; that is, any thing outside of the Five Points [of theology]; but I think that this resolution is eminently befitting this public occasion.

The American Bible Society was organized after the war of 1812, and took the Word of God in hand, and rolled its peaceful offices along the shores of the Atlantic; and now at the close of another war you are required to take this blessed Word in your hands and spread it faithfully over the wild prairies of the West, that were scarcely known and not peopled at that time, and down over our Southern States, to rejuvenate them and to proclaim to them all a new day of peace, of brotherly love and Christian sympathy, of holy earnestness in spreading the Word of our blessed Master, not only over this continent, but to the utmost ends of the earth. It is eminently befitting that you should realize this at this time, and crowd yourselves anew to the work, so that before another fifty years have rolled away there may be a blessed record given of it, not only in this land, but throughout the whole world. Go faithfully then, sir, to this work; take that blessed Word in your hand, and it will do more to reconstruct these sundered States, and to renew this society that has been so dislocated, and to bring back the very spirit of brotherly love, than all the legislation in the world. It is your work, it is our work, to do this; and therefore I second this resolution with all my heart. It is the appropriate resolution on this Jubilee occasion.

Reference has been made to the Jubilee of the British and Foreign Bible Society, when Bishop M'Ilvaine and I were honoured to be your delegates to speak on that occasion; and now we have representatives here, Englishmen, to speak on this occasion. Do you suppose that Earl Russell has had any thing to do with this delegation? I would advise Mr. Seward to have his eye upon it, because he could not, if he had sent all the diplomats in Great Britain, have done more than he has done to cheat us out of our Christian wrath. I am sure there is some diplomacy in this; but, Mr. President, I will say this, in the spreading of that Bible, and acting upon the principles of mutual respect and mutual right, may these two Protestant nations of the world be bound henceforth and for ever in the bonds of amity; and, sir, fulfilling our obligations as the Protestant nations of the world, may we be prepared to go forth shoulder to shoulder in spreading the blessed light, and truth, and principles of liberty, and the everlasting salvation, and the good hope through Christ, that are contained in this Word of God, until it shall bless all nations that dwell upon the face of the earth. This is my sentiment, and I hope our brethren will bear it back (I think it is the sentiment of this whole assembly, as I know it is of the Society) to the British and Foreign Bible Society.

Major-General Howard, U. S. Army, moved the adoption of the following resolution:

Resolved, That we regard with patriotic and Christian interest the supply of the South with the Holy Scriptures, without respect of race or colour, and that we hail with satisfaction the increasing spirit of co-operation manifested by the friends of the Bible throughout that region of our common country.

The address of General Howard consisted mainly of a large mass of testimony from official sources respecting the condition of the freedmen of the South. The great length of this production compels us to select only those passages which bore immediately upon the object and work of the American Bible Society.

Commencing with a graceful allusion to his military position during the war, and his being called to "bring up the rear" of the array of speakers on this occasion, the general proceeded:

The grand object of this honoured Association, the American Bible Society, is the extension of Christ's earthly kingdom and the promotion of true religion. It is found altogether practicable in the furtherance of these objects to circulate the Holy Scriptures, sending them into all the world, that they may preach the Gospel to every creature.

Much seed, we know, falls by the way side upon hardened ground, where it can take no root; much, also, upon stony soil, where no fruit comes to maturity; but nevertheless a goodly portion does fall upon good ground, and bears fruit varying immeasurably in amount according to the locality and the preparation of the soil.

The attention of the Society has been, of late, called to the recent slave States. It is this locality, as one demanding unusual preparation and a careful sowing of Bible seed, that I ask this Society to visit and most thoroughly explore.

Every variety of circumstance and condition that pertains to mankind will be found there—wealth, culture, taste, elegance, contentment, comfort, competence, scarcity, poverty, and suffering: every grade of intellectual developement, from the ripe scholar to the most degraded and ignorant of human beings. With no disposition to awaken any old feelings of sectional pride, but for the sake of the remedy, let me state that at the beginning of this war upwards of six hundred thousand white adults and upwards of three millions of blacks in the late slave States could neither read nor write. I do not suppose that all these people are without Bibles; on the contrary, many of them were preached to on the Sabbath, many heard the Scriptures read, and, though necessarily ignorant, a large number did catch the spirit of the Gospel, and exercise a simple faith and practice that may put to the blush those of us who have enjoyed exalted privileges from childhood.

Yet, with all this, after you have taken a few model plantations, where the master and mistress believed in the manhood of the slave, and embraced all the religious instructions dealt out to the negroes—after you have carefully estimated the numbers of real Christians amongst the poor and despised whites, you cannot but feel that thousands of fields are still rough and stony—that much soil is not yet broken up at all, or prepared for a promising seed-time or a prospective harvest.

Then, after dwelling upon the fact that slavery has ceased throughout the land, he gave his testimony respecting the present condition of the freedmen, "under the three heads, Labour, Education, Justice."

We give the principal statements respecting education, as this subject is so intimately connected with that of the circulation of the Word of God among the freed people:

My school inspector's report for January 1st of this year makes the whole number of scholars in the late slave States, excepting Delaware and including the District of Columbia, 90,589; teachers, 1,314; schools, 740. This does not include the regiments of coloured soldiers, all of which were more or less favoured with opportunities for learning to read while in the service. One large regiment came to my knowledge where every man learned to read and write.

I will recite what the same inspector says of schools in Mississippi, as a sample of the condition of such matters in the South: "There is a mixture of good and evil to report from this State. Your officers are indefatigable in their efforts. There are many good schools among the thirty-four in operation. Some of them have made admirable progress, and a number not included have started under various auspices in different parts of the State. There is every where the usual eagerness to learn. But in some sections inveterate opposition among the whites is manifested towards these schools. Two teachers, at the time I was there, were sent to one of the large towns, twenty-five miles into the country, where there was no military, and the next morning they were ordered off, and threatened if they did not go. This opposition is often openly avowed, but more generally is tacit and concealed, making itself felt every where in a sort of combination not to allow the freedmen any place in which a school may be taught." A superintendent in an interior town says, "The opposition to negro education is very great in my town and neighbourhood." Coloured men, in some instances, have paid their own money to prepare and furnish a room for a school, and then have been forbidden to use it, the white people taking it from them for their own children. Similiar things are true of other States, though in Mississippi such opposition has seemed to be more common than elsewhere; and yet there are redeeming features. Instances of planters have come to our knowledge who are desirous of employing teachers for the freed people. One of your officers states that "many planters are beginning to perceive that schools for the children would be an inducement for labourers to engage with them." General opposition is undoubtedly decreasing. We notice expressions of hope from those who are labouring in the State, and it is clear that a steady system of effort cannot be resisted; as I told one of the planters, "They would find it harder fighting the alphabet and spelling-book than they did Grant and Sherman." He made no reply.

There are now sixty-eight teachers in the State, thirty-four schools, and 4,310 enrolled pupils. More than half of these are considerably advanced in reading, writing, and arithmetic.

In the department of Washington there are sixty-three freedmen's schools, and upwards of 6,000 pupils. Some 5,000 of these are good readers, learning also grammar, geography, arithmetic, and sometimes higher branches; 2,304 are learning to write; 825 are still in the alphabet. Besides these there are sixteen night schools and a large number of Sabbath schools.

A number of industrial schools have been started, one of which made during the last month 162 garments; another, 100 articles of clothing.

With regard to the schools of the district the superintendent says, "All the teachers seem to be earnest and hopeful." One writes: "I find the children are very much like white ones—some stupid and others bright. They are now rather more eager for learning, because it has been fruit forbidden to them." The inspector adds further, that there are large numbers attending some sort of schools of a voluntary or self-supporting character that are not reported. Throughout the entire South an effort is being made by the coloured people to educate themselves. In the absence of other teaching, they are determined to be self-taught, and every where some elementary text-book or the fragment of one may be seen in the hands of negroes. They quickly communicate to each other, so that with very little learning many take to teaching.

A willingness, even an ambition, to bear expenses is also noticed. They often say, "We want to show how much we can do ourselves, if you will only give us a chance."

This may seem an overstatement to those who doubt the character of the negro; not that they are ungrateful or unwilling to be helped, but so universal is the feeling I am describing, that it seems as if some unseen influence was inspiring them to that intelligence which they now so immediately need. Not only are individuals seen at study, and under the most untoward circumstances, but in very many places I found what I may call *native schools;* often rude and very imperfect, but *there they are,* a group perhaps of all ages, *trying to learn.* Some young man, some woman, or old preacher, in cellar, or shed, or corner of a negro meeting-house, with the alphabet in hand or a torn spelling book, is their teacher. All are full of enthusiasm with the new knowledge the book is imparting to them.

All the statistics of this inspector's report are corroborated by the different assistant commissioners and agents of the Freedmen's Bureau. The educational advantages are not confined to the freedmen; schools for the poor whites have been established, though as yet there is not a very large number.

The foregoing views are hopeful, sanguine; but the number of teachers must be multiplied by twenty, and the school advantages proportionably increased.

The question constantly occurs, Can this be done against the prejudices of the white people? We need not stop to ask. What joy would have thrilled through our churches, if at any time, in a single year, such immense progress could have been recorded in any missionary field *abroad.* How gladly they would have put a Bible or Testament into the hands of every new scholar who had become able and willing to read!

The general concluded thus:

During our encampment beneath the celebrated Lookout Mountain, where General Hooker wreathed his brow with fresh laurels, we had opportunity to become familiar with the state of society in that region of country, where all the men remaining at home were *poor whites.* Just opposite my headquarters was a log cabin containing two rooms. At first it was occupied by a poor woman with five or six children. She was half ill, unhappy, discouraged, without learning. Her husband was absent in the rebel army. The cabin was falling in, crevices were open through the sides, and nothing about the premises indicated the first particle of comfort or of cheer. The husband finally came home, thoroughly broken down by his hard campaigning. He had some little knowledge, wished to do right, did not believe in the war; but his future was completely dark, and he added another burden to an already desolate and overburdened household. His children were shrewd, quick to catch new thoughts, but their minds were undeveloped. This picture is a true one of hundreds of others in that region. We established a Sunday school; old and young came to it, and a fountain of joy, and comfort, and hope was found in the Bible, and Bible truths conveyed to these poor people by the army chaplain, the Christian Commission agents, and Christian soldiers. Frequently an old man of seventy years crept down the winding path from the top of the mountain range between us and the river, and begged some return for the corn our soldiers had taken from him. He loved the country, he loved the flag, he loved the Saviour; he made no complaint, but was grateful for the food that God gave him in payment for his toilsome journey, and for the medicines he could take to his poor, sick wife. I visited his home. No country can furnish a rougher dwelling place. It would have been hard for him to find soil enough to plant his corn had it not been taken from him. Oh, the desolation of that house! His wife was a much younger woman than himself, but her health was gone. She was lying on a sort of couch, that answered the name of bed; her face was turned away from the door; she was so still, her hand and cheek seemed so livid, that at first I thought she was dead. This bed, with perhaps two broken chairs, constituted all the furniture. The old man sat quietly in the doorway, and greeted me joyously. He had a part of a Bible. He could not read much himself, but managed to study out a few of the precious truths. His wife aroused herself from her apparent lethargy, and talked to me of Christ, and showed me how some faithful messenger of the Lord had found her and opened to her the wellspring of eternal life. Talk of hate of the negroes! It was not there in all that region. At least I did not discover it.

Their mountains are rich in minerals; their valleys will one day be filled with grain, and fruits, and flowers. That river, the beautiful, graceful, winding Tennessee, will one day be freighted with precious ores and rich products of the soil. The railroad which runs over the top of the mountains and curves backwards and forwards through their deep valleys and gorges, and which, in war, could supply daily two hundred thousand men, when it was infested by guerrillas, when train after train was obstructed, thrown off embankments, broken up, burned up, or otherwise molested; when the track was often torn up, sometimes from ten to twenty miles in extent, the ties consumed and the iron twisted or bent double—that same railroad will one day joyously supply a teeming, thriving, prosperous people. It will be when every vestige of slavery shall have disappeared, and when the loyalty of the North and West shall be firmly linked to that of East Tennessee; linked together in the pursuit of moral, intellectual, and physical wealth, vastly strengthened by the true linking, which is the Bible and the diffusion of such Bible truths as that "love worketh no ill to his neighbour," that "love is the fulfilling of the law." It will be when the Christian can open his heart to the full sunlight, that his heart may expand above, below, around, till he can like Christ, hi Master, *love* man as man, and be willing to protect and bless him, whether he lives in the valley or on the mountain top, whether he be wise or unwise, whether he be black or white.

Prejudice, passion, falsehood, malignancy, and hate, do commingle in the human soul like a sea, turbulent and seething with a fearful power of fiendish life. Thus evil spirits must be allayed; nay, they must be expelled. It can be done only by the spread of Gospel truth. This truth will change the face of things completely in the Southern States. The proud will be brought low, the poor whites will be raised up, the load of ignorance and superstition will be lifted from them and also from the negroes, and real peace will follow, will be pure, and will prevail.

Rev. Dr. Jonas King, of Athens, Greece, seconded the resolution, and said:

All honour to such a noble and splendid general. As for me, I am simply a soldier. I have been a soldier for nearly fifty years. I have been in some battles, and fought in Egypt near the pyramids, and in Palestine and Asia Minor. I was once a missionary in South Carolina and know something of the blacks. I have had a chance to know something of the influence of the Word of God, not only among the poor slaves, but also in the palaces of the kings of Europe. To say that it is a happy influence is to say what every one must know to be true. I consider that the Bible is the centre of the moral world, as the sun is the centre of the natural world. The missionary societies are as the moons, and the tract societies as the stars, of this grand and moral universe. The Queen of England was once asked by some African prince, to what England owes her greatness and prosperity. In answer she showed him the Bible. The longer I observe its influence, the more thoroughly am I convinced of the importance of the Bible. It is enough; it is sufficient. Let us then do all that can be done to put a Bible in the hands of every man, woman, and child in the whole world.

The Rev. Mark Hopkins, D.D., of Mass., pronounced the benediction, and the Society adjourned.

OFFICERS OF THE AMERICAN BIBLE SOCIETY.

President.

JAMES LENOX, Esq., New York.

Vice Presidents.

HON. HEMAN LINCOLN, Massachusetts.
" JOAQUIN MOSQUERA, New Granada.
THOMAS COCK, M.D., New York.
HON. PETER D. VROOM, New Jersey.
JOHN TAPPAN, Esq., Massachusetts.
GEN. JOHN H. COCKE, Virginia.
ARISTARCHUS CHAMPION, Esq., New York.
HON. ALLEN TRIMBLE, Ohio.
FREEBORN GARRETSON, Esq., New York.
HON. W. W. ELLSWORTH, Connecticut.
" EDWARD M'GEHEE, Mississippi.,
" A. B. HASBROUCK, New York.
" R. H. WALWORTH, New York.
FRANCIS HALL, Esq., New York.
MYRON PHELPS, Esq., Illinois.
JAMES A. MAYBIN, Esq., Louisiana.
HON. DAVID L. SWAIN, North Carolina.
" JOSEPH H. LUMPKIN, Georgia.
" JOSEPH A. WRIGHT, Indiana.
" JACOB SLEEPER, Massachusetts.
FREDERICK T. FRELINGHUYSEN, Esq., New Jersey.
WILLIAM WHITLOCK, Jr., Esq., New York.
HON. ROBERT C. WINTHROP, Massachusetts.
" WILLIAM A. BUCKINGHAM, Connecticut.
" SALMON P. CHASE, Ohio.
NORMAN WHITE, Esq., New York.
FREDERICK S. WINSTON, Esq., New York.
GEN. WILLIAM WILLIAMS, Connecticut.
HON. GRANT GOODRICH, Illinois.
JAMES SUYDAM, Esq., New York.
GEORGE H. STUART, Esq., Pennsylvania.

Secretaries.

REV JOSEPH HOLDICH, D.D.
" WM. J. R. TAYLOR, D.D.
" T. RALSTON SMITH.

Treasurer.

WILLIAM WHITLOCK, Jr.

Assistant Treasurer.

HENRY FISHER.

General Agent.

CALEB T. ROWE.

MANAGERS.

First Class.

TERM—1866 to 1870.

FREDERICK T. PEET.
ISAAC WOOD, M. D.
CORNELIUS DU BOIS.
WASHINGTON R. VERMILYE.
E. J. WOOLSEY.
ROBERT CARTER.
MARSHALL S. BIDWELL.
CHANDLER STARR.
RICHARD P. BUCK.

Second Class.

TERM—1865 to 1869.

RICHARD T. HAINES.
JAMES DONALDSON.
CHARLES N. TALBOT.
A. P. CUMINGS.
WM. H. ASPINWALL.
JOHN DAVID WOLFE.
SCHUREMAN HALSTED.
E. L. FANCHER.
WM. G. LAMBERT.

Third Class.

TERM—1864 to 1868.

RALPH MEAD.
JAMES W. DOMINICK.
ARCHIBALD RUSSELL.
FREDERICK H. WOLCOTT.
WILLIAM E. DODGE.
HENRY J. BAKER.
WILLIAM H. CROSBY.
NATHAN BISHOP.
HENRY DICKINSON.

Fourth Class.

TERM—1863 to 1867.

JAMES L. PHELPS, M.D.
GEORGE D. PHELPS.
CHARLES TRACY.
G. P. DISOSWAY.
A. ROBERTSON WALSH.
ALFRED EDWARDS.
ALEXANDER VAN RENSSELAER.
JONATHAN STURGES.
HIRAM M. FORRESTER.

STANDING COMMITTEES

OF THE

AMERICAN BIBLE SOCIETY, FIFTY-FIRST YEAR.

Versions.

REV. JOHN N. M'LEOD, D.D., New York.
REV. HENRY B. SMITH, D.D., "
REV. WM. H. CAMPBELL, D.D., New Brunswick, N. J.
REV. HENRY I. SCHMIDT, D.D., New York.
REV. WILLIAM R. WILLIAMS, D.D., "
REV. THEODORE D. WOOLSEY, LL.D., New Haven, Conn.
REV. WM. G. T. SHEDD, D.D., New York.
REV. ARCHIBALD FOSS, New York.
REV. ALEXANDER H. VINTON, D.D., New York.

Finance.

FREDERICK S. WINSTON.
NORMAN WHITE.
A. P. CUMINGS.
W. R. VERMILYE.
WM. G. LAMBERT.
WM. H. CROSBY.
HIRAM M. FORRESTER.

Publication.

FRANCIS HALL.
FREDERICK T. PEET.
RALPH MEAD.
A. ROBERTSON WALSH.
ROBERT CARTER.
CHARLES N. TALBOT.
ALFRED EDWARDS.

Distribution.

REV. ISAAC FERRIS, D.D.
JAMES L. PHELPS, M.D.
FREDERICK H. WOLCOTT
MARSHALL S. BIDWELL.
REV. JOHN COTTON SMITH, D.D.
REV. CHAS. F. E. STOHLMANN, D.D.
REV. WILLIAM ROBERTS, D.D.

Agencies.

REV. THOMAS DE WITT, D.D.
REV. JOHN M. KREBS, D.D.
JAMES W. DOMINICK.
REV. WILLIAM R. TOMPKINS.
REV. THOMAS S. HASTINGS.
NATHAN BISHOP, LL.D.
REV. ALBERT S. HUNT.

Legacies.

CHARLES TRACY.
ISAAC WOOD, M.D.
JAMES SUYDAM.
ALEXANDER VAN RENSSELAER.
WM. H. ASPINWALL.
HENRY DICKINSON.
SCHUREMAN HALSTED.

Nomination.

JAMES SUYDAM.
NORMAN WHITE.
ISAAC WOOD, M.D.
E. L. FANCHER.
RICHARD P. BUCK.
REV. HENRY E. MONTGOMERY, D.D.
CHARLES N. TALBOT.

Anniversaries.

REV. EDMUND S. JANES, D.D.
REV. WILLIAM ADAMS, D.D.
REV. M. S. HUTTON, D.D.
REV. W. I. BUDINGTON, D.D.
REV. ALEXANDER H. VINTON, D.D.
REV. N. L. RICE, D.D.
REV. PHILIP SCHAFF, D.D.

Auditing Committee.

FREDERICK T. PEET.
RICHARD T. HAINES.
SCHUREMAN HALSTED.

CONSTITUTION

OF THE

AMERICAN BIBLE SOCIETY.

ARTICLE I.

This Society shall be known by the name of the AMERICAN BIBLE SOCIETY, of which the sole object shall be to encourage a wider circulation of the Holy Scriptures, without note or comment. The only copies in the English language, to be circulated by the Society, shall be of the version now in common use.

ARTICLE II.

This Society shall add its endeavours to those employed by other societies, for circulating the Scriptures throughout the United States and their Territories; and shall furnish them with stereotype plates, or such other assistance as circumstances may require. This Society shall also, according to its ability, extend its influence to other countries, whether Christian, Mohammedan, or Pagan.

ARTICLE III.

All Bible Societies shall be allowed to purchase, at cost, from this Society, Bibles for distribution within their own districts; and the officers of all such Bible Societies as shall hereafter agree to place their surplus revenue, after supplying their own districts with the Bible, at the disposal of this Society, shall be entitled to vote in all meetings of the Society.

ARTICLE IV.

Each subscriber of three dollars annually shall be a member.

ARTICLE V.

Each subscriber of thirty dollars at one time shall be a member for life.

ARTICLE VI.

Each subscriber of one hundred and fifty dollars at one time, or who shall, by one additional payment, increase his original subscription to one hundred and fifty dollars, shall be a director for life.

ARTICLE VII.

Directors shall be entitled to attend and vote at all meetings of the Board of Managers.

ARTICLE VIII.

A Board of Managers shall be appointed to conduct the business of the Society, consisting of thirty-six laymen, of whom twenty-four shall reside in the city of New York or its vicinity. One fourth part of the whole number shall go out of office at the expiration of each year, but shall be re-eligible.

Every Minister of the Gospel, who is a member for life of the Society, shall be entitled to meet and vote with the Board of Managers, and be possessed of the same powers as a Manager himself.

The Managers shall appoint all officers, and call special general meetings, and fill such vacancies as may occur, by death or otherwise, in their own Board.

ARTICLE IX.

Each member of the Society shall be entitled, under the direction of the Board of Managers, to purchase Bibles and Testaments at the Society's prices, which shall be as low as possible.

ARTICLE X.

The annual meetings of the Society shall be held at New York or Philadelphia, at the option of the Society, on the second Thursday of May, in each year; when the Managers shall be chosen, the accounts presented, and the proceedings of the foregoing year reported.

ARTICLE XI.

The President, Vice Presidents, Secretaries, Treasurer, Assistant Treasurer, and General Agent, for the time being, shall be considered, *ex officio*, members of the Board of Managers.

ARTICLE XII.

At the general meetings of the Society, and the meetings of the Managers, the President, or, in his absence, the Vice President first on the list then present, and in the absence of all the Vice Presidents, such member as shall be appointed for that purpose, shall preside at the meeting.

ARTICLE XIII.

The Managers shall meet on the first Thursday in each month, or oftener if necessary, at such place in the city of New York as they shall from time to time adjourn to.

ARTICLE XIV.

The Managers shall have the power of appointing such persons as have rendered essential services to the Society, either members for life, or directors for life.

ARTICLE XV.

The whole minutes of every meeting shall be signed by the Chairman.

ARTICLE XVI.

No alteration shall be made in this Constitution, except by the Society at an annual meeting, on the recommendation of the Board of Managers.

ARTICLE XVII.

The President, or, in his absence, the Vice President first on the list in the city of New York, *may*, and on the written request of six members of the Board, *shall* call a special meeting of the Board of Managers, giving three days' notice of such meeting, and of its object.

ARTICLE XVIII.

The Board of Managers may admit to the privileges of an Auxiliary any society which was organized, and had commenced the printing, publication, and issuing of the Sacred Scriptures before the establishment of this Society, with such relaxation of the terms of admission heretofore prescribed, as the said Board, two thirds of the members present consenting, may think proper.

Notices to Auxiliaries.

The American Bible Society is now in a situation to furnish all their Auxiliaries, and other Bible Societies, with any quantity of well printed and well bound Bibles and Testaments at the shortest notice.

Auxiliaries are requested to be very particular in sending their Annual Reports, names of Officers, etc., etc.

Whenever a new society is organized, notice of the event should be given *immediately* to the Parent Society, so that it may be recognised. The names of its officers and their post-office addresses should also be given.

⁎ Particular care should be taken to send the information requisite to their being recognised; for which see the cover of Annual Report, head, "New Auxiliary Societies."

Correspondence, etc.

Pecuniary Remittances, and letters in relation to the accounts of Agents, Auxiliary and other Societies and persons, and legacies, should be addressed to Henry Fisher, Assistant Treasurer, Bible House, Astor Place, New York.

Letters relating to Travelling Agencies, to Delegations for Auxiliary Anniversaries, and inquiries as to the mode of raising funds, requests for *donations* of books, inquiries as to the general policy of the Society, notice of new Auxiliaries formed, reports of those already recognised, and communications for the Record, should be directed to "Secretaries of the American Bible Society," Bible House, Astor Place, New York.

Orders for Books, and letters in relation to the transmission of Reports and Records, should be directed to Caleb T. Rowe, General Agent, Bible House, Astor Place, New York.

The Board of Managers beg leave to state that it is very desirable that orders for books should be accompanied WITH PAYMENT, it being understood that the moneys are usually collected by societies previous to their purchasing books. Such is the demand upon the Depository, that long credits prevent the Parent Institution from receiving the benefit of the DISCOUNT allowed for prompt payment in the purchase of PAPER and other materials.

www.ingramcontent.com/pod-product-compliance
Lightning Source LLC
Chambersburg PA
CBHW030622270326
41927CB00007B/1283

* 9 7 8 3 3 3 7 0 9 9 9 4 7 *